the SPANISH
TRAVELMATE

Compiled by Lexus
with Alicia de Benito de Harland
and Mike Harland

Chronicle Books · San Francisco

Cover design: Kathy Warinner
Composition: TBH Typecast

ISBN: 0-87701-869-3

10 9 8 7 6 5 4 3 2 1

Chronicle Books
275 Fifth Street
San Francisco, California 94103

YOUR TRAVELMATE
gives you one single easy-to-use list of useful
words and phrases to help you communicate in
Spanish.

Built into this list are:
– Travel Tips with facts and figures which
provide valuable information
– Spanish words you'll see on signs and notices
– typical replies to some of the things you might
want to say.

There is a menu reader on pages 70–71 and
numbers and the Spanish alphabet are given on
pages 124–125.

Your TRAVELMATE also tells you how to
pronounce Spanish. Just read the pronunciations
as though they were English and you will
communicate – although you might not sound like
a native speaker.

One special sound:
h is like the ch in Scottish "loch"

If no pronunciation is given then the word itself
can be spoken as though it were English. And
sometimes only part of a word or phrase needs a
pronunciation guide. Vowels in italics show which
part of a word to stress.

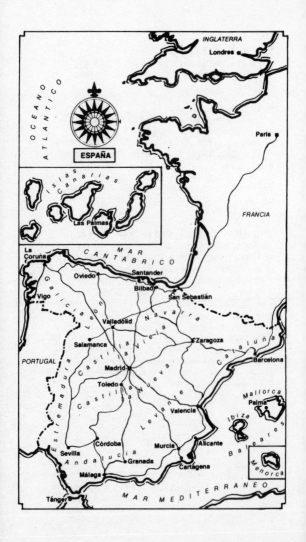

a, an un; una [oon, oona]
  70 pesetas a liter setenta pesetas el litro
abdomen el abdomen [abdoh-men]
abierto open
aboard a bordo
  about: about 15 unos quince [oonoss keentheh]
  about 2 o'clock sobre las dos [soh-breh]
above por encima [por entheema]
  above that por encima de eso
abroad en el extranjero [estranheh-roh]
absolutely! ¡desde luego! [dezdeh lweh-goh]
accelerator el acelerador [atheh-lerador]
accept aceptar [atheptar]
accident un accidente [aktheedenteh]
  there's been an accident ha habido un accidente [ah abeedoh oon . . .]
accommodation alojamiento [aloham-yentoh]
  we need accommodation for three necesitamos alojamiento para tres personas [nethesseetah-moss . . .]
» *TRAVEL TIP: apart from hotels there are also three categories of "pensión" (boarding house) often cheaper and quite adequate with meals available*
accurate exacto [eggs-aktoh]
ache un dolor
  it aches me duele [meh dweh-leh]
across al otro lado
  how do we get across? ¿cómo se cruza? [. . . krootha]

....

across the street al otro lado de la calle
[...ka-yeh]
adapter un adapta*r*
address la dirección [deerekth-yon]
  will you give me your address? ¿me quiere
  dar su dirección? [meh kee-eh-reh...]
adhesive bandage una tirita [teereeta]
admission la entra*a*
advance: can we reserve in advance? ¿se
  pueden hacer las reservas por adelantado? [seh
  pweh-den ath-air...]
advertisement un anuncio [anoon-thee-oh]
afraid: I'm afraid I don't know me temo que
  no lo sé [meh teh-moh keh noh loh seh]
  I'm afraid so me temo que sí
  I'm afraid not me temo que no
after: after you usted primero [oosteh...]
  after 2 o'clock después de las dos [dess-pwess]
afternoon la tarde [tar-deh]
  in the afternoon por la tarde
  good afternoon buenas tardes [bweh-nass
  tardess]
  this afternoon esta tarde
aftershave "aftershave"
again otra vez [oh-tra veth]
against contra
age edad [eh-da]
  under age menor de edad
  it takes ages se tarda mucho [moochoh]
ago: a week ago hace una semana [ah-theh
  oona seh-mah-na]
  it wasn't long ago no hace mucho tiempo
  [noh ah-theh moochoh tee-empoh]
  how long ago was that? ¿cuánto tiempo hace
  de eso? [kwantoh...ah-theh...]
agree: I agree estoy de acuerdo [...akwair-
  doh]; **it doesn't agree with me** no me sienta
  bien [noh meh see-enta bee-en]
agua potable drinking water
air aire [eye-reh]
  by air en avión [av-yon]

by airmail por avión
with air-conditioning con aire acondicionado [–deeth-yon*a*h-doh]
airport el aeropuerto [ah-airoh-pw*a*ir-toh]
alarm la alarma
  alarm clock un despertador
alcohol alcohol [alko-ol]
  is it alcoholic? ¿tiene alcohol? [tee-*e*h-neh . . .]
alive vivo [v*ee*–]
  is he still alive? ¿vive todavía? [v*ee*-veh toh-dav*ee*-ah]
all todo [t*o*h-doh]
  all night toda la noche [t*o*h-da la n*o*tcheh]
  that's all wrong está todo mal
  all right de acuerdo [deh akw*a*ir-doh]
  I'm all right est*o*y bien [. . . bee-*e*n]
  that's all eso es todo
  thank you – not at all gracias – de nada [gr*a*th-yass-deh n*a*h-da]
allergic al*é*rgico [al*a*ir-*h*eekoh]
  I'm allergic to . . . soy al*é*rgico a . . .
allowed permitido
  is it allowed? ¿est*á* perm*í*tido?
  allow me perm*í*tame [pair-m*ee*ta-meh]
almost casi [k*a*h-see]
alone solo
  did you come here alone? ¿ha venido solo? [ah . . .]
  leave me alone d*é*jeme en paz [d*e*hemeh em path]
alquiler de coches car rental *service*
already ya
also tambi*é*n [tamb-y*e*n]
alternator un alternador [al-tair-nad*o*r]
although aunque [*o*wng-keh]
alto halt
altogether del todo
  what does that make altogether? ¿cuánto es en tot*a*l? [kw*a*ntoh . . .]
always siempre [see-*e*m-preh]

a.m. de la mañana [. . . man-yah-na] *(in conversation)* In timetables the 24-hour system is used.

ambassador el embajador [emba-*h*ador]

ambulance una ambulancia [ambool*a*nthee-a]
  get an ambulance! ¡llame a una ambulancia! [y*a*h-meh . . .]

» *TRAVEL TIP: not always available: advisable to use a car and race to hospital waving a white handkerchief out of window and blaring horn*

America América

American americano

among entre [entreh]

amps amperios [amp*e*h-ree-oss]
  15-amp fuse un fusible de quince amperios [foo-s*e*e-bleh deh k*e*entheh . . .]

anchor el ancla

and y [ee]

andén platform

angry enfadado
  I'm very angry about it estoy muy [mwee] enfadado por ello [*e*h-yoh]
  please don't get angry haga [*a*h-ga] el favor de no enfadarse [emfad*a*r-seh]

animal un anim*a*l

ankle el tobillo [toh-b*e*e-yoh]

anniversary: it's our anniversary es nuestro aniversario [. . . nw*e*ss-troh . . .]

annoy: he's annoying me me est*á* molestando [m*e*h . . .]
  it's very annoying es muy molesto [mwee]

another: can we have another room? ¿puede d*a*rnos otra habitación? [pw*e*h-deh . . . abbeetath-y*o*n]
  another beer, please por fav*o*r, otra cerveza [. . . thair-v*e*h-tha]

answer: what was his answer? ¿qué respondió? [keh respond-y*o*h]
  there was no answer no hubo respuesta [. . . *o*oboh ress-pw*e*ss-ta]

antifreeze anticongelante [anti-kon*h*ell*a*nteh]

any: have you got any bananas/butter? ¿tiene
usted plátanos/mantequilla? [tee-*eh*-neh
oosteh . . . manteh-k*ee*ya]
I haven't got any no tengo
anybody cualquiera [kwal-kee-*eh*-ra]
can anybody help? ¿alguien puede ayudar?
[*a*l-ghee-en pweh-deh ah-yoo-d*a*r]
anything algo
I don't want anything no quiero nada
[. . . kee-*eh*-roh . . .]
apartment: I'm looking for an
apartment estoy buscando un piso
[. . . p*ee*-soh]
aparcamiento parking lot
aperitif un aperitivo [−t*ee*−]
apology una disculpa
please accept my apologies por favor, acepte
mis disculpas [. . . ath*e*pteh meess . . .]
I want an apology quiero que me pida
disculpas [kee-*eh*-roh keh meh p*ee*da . . .]
appendicitis apendicitis [−th*ee*-teess]
appetite apetito [−t*ee*−]
I've lost my appetite he perdido el apetito
[eh pair-d*ee*doh el apeh-t*ee*-toh]
apple una manzana [man-th*a*h-na]
application form un impreso de solicitud
[. . . eempr*e*h-soh deh soleeth*ee*t*oo*]
appointment una cita [th*ee*−]
can I make an appointment? *(with*
doctor) quería pedir hora [ker*ee*-a ped*ee*r *o*ra]
apricot un albaricoque [albareek*o*keh]
April abril [abr*ee*l]
archaeology arqueología [arkeh-ollo-*hee*-a]
area la zona [th*o*na]
arm el brazo [−th−]
around: is he around? ¿está por aquí?
[. . . ak*ee*]
arrange: will you arrange it? ¿lo arreglará
usted? [. . . oost*e*h]
it's all arranged todo está arreglado

arrest *(verb)* detener [deh-ten*air*]
  he's been arrested le han detenido [leh an
  deh-ten*ee*doh]
arrival la llegada [yeh-g*a*h-da]
arrive llegar [yeh-g*a*r]
  we only arrived yesterday llegamos tan sólo
  ayer [yeh-g*a*h-moss . . . ah-y*a*ir]
art el arte [−t*e*h]
art gallery museo de bellas artes [moo-s*e*h-oh
  deh b*e*h-yass *a*rtess]
arthritis artritis [ar-tr*ee*-teess]
artificial artificial [arteefeeth-y*a*l]
artist un pintor [peen-t*o*r]
as: as quickly as you can lo más de prisa que
  pueda [loh mass deh pr*ee*-sa keh pw*e*h-da]
  as much as you can tanto como pueda
  [. . . pw*e*h-da]
  do as I do haga como yo [*a*h-ga . . .]
  as you like como usted quiera [. . . oost*e*h
  kee-*e*h-ra]
ascensor elevator
aseos toilets
ashore: to go ashore desembarc*a*r
ashtray un cenicero [thenee-th*e*h-roh]
ask pregunt*a*r
  I didn't ask for that no había pedido eso [no
  ab*ee*-a ped*ee*doh *e*h-soh]
  could you ask him to . . . ? ¿podría pedirle
  que . . . ? [pod-r*ee*-a ped*ee*r-leh keh]
asleep: he's still asleep todavía está durmiendo
  [todav*ee*-a est*a* door-mee-*e*n-doh]
asparagus un esp*á*rrago
aspirin una aspirina [asspeer*ee*na]
assistant un ayudante [ah-yoo-d*a*nteh]
  (shop) un dependiente [−dee-*e*nteh]
asthma asma [*a*zma]
at: at the cafe en el caf*é*
  at my hotel en mi hotel [. . . mee oh-t*e*ll]
atención al tren beware of trains
atmosphere la atmósfera [atmoss-f*e*h-ra]
attitude una actitud [akteet*oo*]

attractive guapa [gwah-pa]
  I think you're very attractive me pareces
  muy guapa [meh pareh-thess mwee gwah-pa]
August agosto [agoss-toh]
aunt: my aunt mi tía [mee tee-a]
Australia Australia [ows-trah-lee-a]
Australian australiano [−yah-noh]
authorities las autoridades [ow-torree-dah-dess]
automatic *(car)* automático [owtoh−]
autopista *freeway*
autoservicio *self-service*
autumn otoño [oh-tohn-yoh]
  in the autumn en otoño
away: is it far away from here? ¿está muy
  lejos de aquí? [. . . mwee leh-hoss deh akee]
  go away! ¡lárguese! [largheh-seh]
awful terrible [terree-bleh]
axle el eje [eh-heh]
baby un bebé [beh-beh]
  we'd like a baby-sitter quisiéramos una baby-
  sitter [keess-yeh-ramoss . . .]
back: I've got a bad back padezco de dolor de
  espalda [padeth-koh . . .]
  I'll be back soon estaré de vuelta pronto
  [esstareh deh vwelta . . .]
  can I have my money back? ¿me puede
  devolver el importe? [meh pweh-deh deh-
  volvair . . . -teh]
  come back! ¡vuelva! [vwelva]
  I go back tomorrow me vuelvo mañana
  [meh . . .]
  at the back por detrás
backpack una mochila [-chee-]
bacon bacon
  bacon and eggs huevos con bacon [weh-voss . . .]
bad malo; **it's not bad** no está mal
  too bad! ¡qué le vamos a hacer! [keh leh
  vah-moss athair]
  the milk/meat is bad la leche está cortada/la
  carne está pasada [. . . leh-cheh . . . /
   . . . karneh . . .]

....

bag una bolsa
  (handbag, suitcase) un bolso
baggage equipaje [eckee-p*a*h-*h*eh]
bakery la panadería [−*ee*-a]
balcony un balcón
  a room with a balcony una habitación con
  balcón [abbee-tath-y*o*n . . .]
ball una pelota
ballpoint pen un bol*í*grafo
banana un pl*á*tano
band *(mus)* la orquesta [ork*e*ssta]
bandage una venda
  could you change the bandage? ¿quiere
  cambiar el vendaje? [kee-*e*h-reh kambee-*a*r el
  vend*a*h-*h*eh]
  adhesive bandage una tirita [teer*ee*ta]
bank el banco; *(of river)* la orilla [or*ee*-ya]
» *TRAVEL TIP: banking hours: 9-1 Mon-Sat;
  see* **public holidays, change**
bar el bar
  when does the bar open? ¿a qué hora se
  abre el bar? [ah keh *o*ra seh *a*h-breh . . .]
» *TRAVEL TIP: see* **café**
barbershop una peluquería de caballeros
  [pelookeh-r*ee*-a deh kaba-y*e*h-ross]
bargain: it's a real bargain es una verdadera
  ganga [. . . vairda-d*e*h-ra . . .]
bartender el camarero [−r*e*h-roh]
basket un cesto [th−]
bassinet un capazo [kap*a*h-thoh]
bath un baño [b*a*hn-yoh]
  can I have a bath? ¿puedo darme un baño?
  [pw*e*h-doh d*a*r-meh oon . . .]
  could you give me a bath towel? ¿me podría
  dar una toalla de baño? [meh podr*ee*-a dar
  oona toh-*a*h-ya deh . . .]
bathing el baño [b*a*hn-yoh]
  bathing suit traje de baño [tr*a*h-*h*eh deh . . .]
bathrobe una bata
bathroom cuarto de baño [kw*a*rtoh deh
  b*a*hn-yoh]

we want a room with a private bathroom queremos una habitación con cuarto de baño [keh-reh-moss oona abbee-tath-yon kon . . .]

can I use your bathroom? ¿puedo usar su cuarto de baño [pweh-doh oosar soo . . .]

» TRAVEL TIP: see **toilet**

battery la batería [bateh-ree-a]

be ser [sair]

be good sé bueno [seh bweh-noh]

don't be lazy no seas vago [. . . seh-ass vah-goh]

beach la playa [pla-ya]

on the beach en la playa

beans judías [hoodee-ass]

runner beans judías verdes [. . . vair-dess]

dried beans judías blancas

broad beans habas [ah-bass]

beautiful precioso [preth-yoh-soh]

that was a beautiful meal ha sido una comida estupenda [ah see-doh oona kommeeda esstoopenda]

because porque [por-keh]

because of the bad weather debido al mal tiempo [debeedoh . . . tee-empoh]

bed una cama

single bed/double bed cama individual/cama doble [. . . doh-bleh]

bed and breakfast alojamiento y desayuno [alo-ham-yentoh ee dessa-yoonoh]

I want to go to bed quiero acostarme [kee-eh-roh . . . —meh]

bedroom un dormitorio

bee una abeja [abeh-ha]

beef carne de vaca [karneh . . .]

beer cerveza [thairveh-tha]

two beers, please dos cervezas, por favor

» TRAVEL TIP: cerveza implies lager

before: before breakfast antes de desayunar [an-tess deh dessa-yoo-nar]

before we leave antes de marcharnos
I haven't been here before nunca había
estado aquí [noonka ab*ee*-a esst*ah*-doh ak*ee*]
begin: when does it begin? ¿cuándo empieza?
[kw*a*ndoh empee-*e*h-tha]
beginner principiante [preen-theep-y*a*nteh]
beginner's slope *(skiing)* la pista de
principiantes [p*ee*sta deh preen-theep-y*a*ntess]
behind detr*a*s
   the car behind me el coche de detr*a*s de mí
[. . . k*o*tcheh . . .]
believe: I don't believe you no le creo [noh leh
kr*e*h-oh]; **I believe you** le creo
bell *(in hotel, etc.)* el timbre [t*ee*m-breh]
belong: that belongs to me eso es mío
   whom does this belong to? ¿de quién es
esto? [deh kee-*e*n ess *e*sstoh]
below abajo [ab*a*h-*h*oh]
belt un cinturón [theen−]
bend *(in road)* una curva [k*o*orva]
berries bayas [b*a*-yass]
berth *(on ship)* una litera [leet-*e*h-ra]
beside junto a [h*oo*ntoh ah]
best el mejor [m*e*hor]
   it's the best vacation I've ever had son las
mejores vacaciones de mi vida [. . . meh*o*ress
vakath-yoness deh mee v*ee*da]
better mejor [m*e*hor]
   haven't you got anything better? ¿no tiene
nada mejor? [noh tee-*e*h-neh . . .]
   are you feeling better? ¿se siente usted
mejor? [seh see-*e*nteh oost*e*h . . .]
   I'm feeling a lot better me siento mucho mejor
between entre [*e*ntreh]
beyond más allá [mass a-y*a*]
   beyond the mountains más allá de las
montañas [. . . mont*a*hn-yass]
bicycle una bicicl*e*ta [beethee-kl*e*h-ta]
   can we hire bicycles here? ¿se pueden
alquilar bicicletas aquí? [seh pw*e*h-den
alkeel*a*r . . . ak*ee*]

bienvenido *welcome*
big grande [−deh]
   a big one uno grande
   that's too big eso es demasiado grande
   [. . . demass-*y*ah-doh . . .]
   it's not big enough no es suficientemente
   grande [. . . soofeeth-*y*enteh-menteh . . .]
have you got a bigger one? ¿tiene usted otro
   más grande? [tee-*e*h-neh oos*t*eh . . .]
bikini un bikini
bill la cuenta [kwenta]
   could I have the bill, please? la cuenta, por
   favor
binding *(ski)* atadura [−d*oo*ra]
bird un pájaro [p*a*-haroh]
birthday cumpleaños [koompleh-*a*n-yoss]
   it's my birthday es mi cumple*a*ños [ess
   mee . . .]
   happy birthday! ¡feliz cumpleaños!
   [fel*ee*th . . .]
bit: just a little bit sólo un poquito [. . . poh-
   k*ee*-toh]
   that's a bit too expensive es un poco caro
   a big bit un pedazo grande [ped*a*h-thoh
   gr*a*ndeh]
   a bit of that cake un pedazo de esa tarta
bite una picadura
   I've been bitten *(insect)* me ha picado un
   bicho [meh ah peek*a*h-doh oon b*ee*choh]
   (dog) me ha mordido un perro [. . . ah
   mord*ee*doh . . .]
bitter *(taste)* amargo
black negro
   he's had a blackout ha sufrido un desmayo
   [ah soofr*e*edoh oon dess-m*a*-yoh]
bland suave [sw*a*h-veh]
blanket una manta
   I'd like another blanket ¿me da otra manta,
   por favor?
bleach lejía [le*hee*-a]
bleed sangrar

....

he's bleeding está sangrando
bless you! *(after sneeze)* ¡Jesús! [*h*eh-s*oo*ss]
blind ciego [thee-*e*h-goh]
  his lights were blinding me me
  deslumbraban sus faros
  blind spot *(driving)* punto ciego [poontoh ...]
blister una ampolla [amp*o*h-ya]
blocked *(pipe)* atascada *(road)* cortada
blonde una rubia [r*oo*b-ya]
blood sangre [s*a*ngreh]
  his blood type is ... su grupo sanguíneo
  es ... [soo gr*oo*poh sang-gh*ee*n-eh-oh]
  I've got high blood pressure tengo la
  tensión alta [... tenss-yon ...]
  he needs a blood transfusion necesita una
  transfusión [nethess*ee*ta oona transf*oo*ss-yon]
Bloody Mary vodka con zumo de tomate
  [... th*oo*moh deh tom*a*h-teh]
blouse una blusa [bl*oo*-sa]
blue azul [ath*oo*l]
board: full board pensión completa [penss-yon
  kompl*e*h-ta]
  half board media pensión [m*ai*d-ya ...]
  boarding pass tarjeta de embarque [tar*h*eh-
  ta de emb*a*rkeh]
boat un barco
body el cuerpo [kw*ai*rpoh]
  dead body un cadáver [−v*air*]
boil hervir; *(medical)* un forúnculo
  do we have to boil the water? ¿es necesario
  hervir el agua? [... nethess*a*r-yoh airv*ee*r el
  *a*hg-wa]
  boiled egg un huevo pasado por agua [oon
  w*e*h-voh ... *a*hg-wa]
bone hueso [w*e*h-soh]
book un libro [l*ee*−]
bookstore una librería [leebreh-r*ee*-a]
boot una bota
border la frontera
bored: I'm bored estoy aburrido
  [... aboorr*ee*doh]

boring aburrido [aboorr*ee*doh]
born: I was born in... nací en... [nath*ee*...]
borrow: can I borrow...? ¿puede
  prestarme...? [pw*eh*-deh... –meh]
boss el jefe [*h*eh-feh]
both los dos
  I'll take both of them me llevo los dos [meh
  y*eh*-voh loss doss]
bottle una botella [bot*eh*-ya]
  bottle opener un abrebotellas [*a*h-breh–]
bottom: at the bottom of the hill al fondo de la
  cuesta [...kw*e*ssta]
bowels el vientre [vee-*e*ntreh]
bowl *(basin)* una palangana
box una caja [k*a*h-*h*a]
boy un chico [ch*ee*koh]
boyfriend: my boyfriend mi amigo [mee
  am*ee*goh]
bra un sostén
bracelet una pulsera [pools*eh*-ra]
brake *(noun)* el freno [fr*eh*-noh]
  could you check the brakes? ¿quiere
  revisarme los frenos? [kee-eh-reh reh-
  vees*a*rmeh loss fr*eh*-noss]
  I had to brake suddenly tuve que frenar
  bruscamente [t*oo*veh keh freh-n*a*r
  brooskam*e*nteh]
  he didn't brake no frenó
brandy coñac [kon-y*a*k]
bread pan
  **could we have some bread and
  butter?** ¿nos pone un poco de pan con
  mantequilla? [...p*o*h-neh...manteh-k*ee*-ya]
  some more bread, please más pan, por favor
break *(verb)* romper [romp-*ai*r]
  I think I've broken my arm me parece que
  me he roto el brazo [meh par*e*h-theh keh meh
  eh r*o*toh el br*a*h-thoh]
breakable frágil [fr*a*h-*h*eel]
breakdown una avería [aveh-r*ee*-a]

nervous breakdown una crisis nerviosa
[kr*eesee*ss nairvee-*osa*]
breakfast el desayuno [dessa-y*oo*noh]
» *TRAVEL TIP: try typical "chocolate con churros,"*
fritters dunked in hot chocolate
breast el pecho
breath aliento [al-y*en*toh]
  he's getting very short of breath se está
  quedando sin resuello [seh est*a* keh-d*a*ndoh
  seen reh-sw*e*ll-yoh]
breathe respirar [resspeer*a*r]
  I can't breathe no puedo respirar [noh
  pw*e*h-doh . . .]
bridge un puente [pw*en*teh]
briefcase la cartera [kart*e*h-ra]
brilliant brillante [bree-y*a*nteh]
bring traer [trah-*air*]
  could you bring it to my hotel? ¿podría
  traérmelo a mi hotel? [podr*ee*-a trah-*air*-meh-
  loh ah mee oh-t*e*l]
Britain Gran Bretaña [. . . bret*a*hn-ya]
British brit*á*nico
brochure un foll*e*to
  have you got any brochures about . . . ?
  ¿tiene usted algún folleto sobre . . . ? [tee-*e*h-neh
  oost*e*h alg*oo*n foyeh-toh soh-breh]
broken roto
  you've broken it lo ha roto usted [loh ah r*o*h-
  toh oost*e*h]
  it's broken est*á* roto
  my room/car has been broken into me han
  desvalijado la habitación/han penetrado en mi
  coche [meh an dess-valee-h*a*h-doh la abbee-
  tath-y*o*n/an . . . mee k*o*tcheh]
brooch un broche [−eh]
brother: my brother mi hermano [mee air-
m*a*h-noh]
brown marr*ó*n; *(tanned)* moreno [mor*e*h-noh]
  brown paper pap*e*l de embal*a*r]
browse: can I just browse around? ¿puedo
echar una ojeada? [pw*e*h-doh . . . oh-*h*e*h*-*a*h-da]

bruise un cardenal
brunette *(noun)* una morena [moreh-na]
brush *(noun)* un cepillo [thep*ee*-yoh]
   (artist's) un pincel [−the*l*]
Brussels sprouts coles de Bruselas [k*o*h-less
   deh broo-s*e*h-lass]
bucket un cubo [k*oo*boh]
buffet un buff*e*t
building un edificio [−f*ee*th-yoh]
bull el toro
   a bull fight una corrida de toros [korree-da
   deh . . .]
bump: he bumped his head se ha dado un
   golpe en la cabeza [seh ah d*a*h-doh oon g*o*lpeh
   en la kab*e*h-tha]
bumper el parachoques [−ch*o*h-kess]
bunk una litera [leet*e*h-ra]
   bunk beds literas
buoy una boya
burglar un ladrón
burned: this meat is burned esta carne est*á*
   quemada [. . . k*a*rneh . . . keh-m*a*h-da]
   my arms are burned me he quemado los
   brazos [meh eh keh-m*a*h-doh loss br*a*h-thoss]
   **can you give me something for these
   burns?** ¿puede darme algo para estas
   quemaduras? [pw*e*h-deh d*a*rmeh . . . keh-
   mad*oo*rass]
bus un autobús [ow-toh-b*oo*ss]
   bus tour un grupo en autocar
   bus stop la parada del autobús
   could you tell me when we get there? ¿hará
   el favor de avisarme cuando lleguemos allí?
   [ar*a* el favor deh avees*a*rmeh kw*a*ndoh yeh-
   gh*e*h-moss a-y*ee*]
business un negocio [neg*o*th-yoh]
   I'm here on business estoy aqui de negocios
   [. . . ak*ee* . . .]
   business trip viaje de negocios [vee-*a*h-*h*eh
   deh neg*o*th-yoss]

none of your business! ¡no es asunto suyo!
[noh ess assoontoh soo-yoh]
bust el pecho
» TRAVEL TIP: *bust measurements*

US	32	34	36	38	40
Spain	80	87	91	97	102

busy ocupado [−koo−]
  (telephone) comunicando [−moo−]
  are you busy? ¿está usted ocupado?
  [. . . oosteh . . .]
but pero [peh-roh]
  not . . . but . . . no . . . sino . . . [seenoh]
butcher shop la carnicería [karneetheh-ree-a]
butter mantequilla [mantekeeya]
button un botón
buy: I'll buy it lo compro
by: I'm here by myself he venido solo [eh
  veneedoh . . .]
  are you by yourself? ¿está usted solo? [esta
  oosteh . . .]
  can you do it by tomorrow? ¿puede tenerlo
  hecho para mañana? [pweh-deh tenairloh
  etchoh . . .]
  by train/car/plane en tren/coche/avión
  I parked by the trees aparqué junto a los
  árboles [aparkeh hoontoh ah loss arboless]
  who's it made by? ¿quién lo fabrica? [kee-en
  loh fabreeka]
caballeros gentlemen
cabaret un cabaret [oon kabareh]
cabbage una col
cabin *(on ship)* un camarote [kamaroh-teh]
cable *(in car, etc.)* un cable [kah-bleh]
café una cafetería [kafeh-teh-ree-a]
» TRAVEL TIP: *cafetería/café/bar all roughly
  equivalent: all sell non-alcoholic and alcoholic
  drinks and snacks; open all day; children
  welcome; cheaper to eat or drink at the bar*
caja cash register
cake un pastel

23

a piece of cake un pedazo de tarta
[peh-d*a*h-thoh]
calculator una calculadora
caliente hot
call: will you call the manager? ¿quiere
llamar al director? [kee-*e*h-reh yam*a*r al
deerekt*o*r]
  what is this called? ¿cómo se llama esto?
calm tranquilo [trank*ee*loh]
  calm down tranquilícese
  [trankee-l*ee*-theh-seh]
camera una máquina de fotos [m*a*keena . . .]
camino cerrado road closed
camp: is there somewhere we can camp?
¿hay algún sitio donde podamos acamp*a*r?
[eye alg*oo*n s*ee*t-yoh . . .]
  can we camp here? ¿se puede acamp*a*r aquí?
  [seh pw*e*h-deh . . . ak*ee*]
  we're on a camping trip estamos de camping
  campsite un camping
» *TRAVEL TIP: camping permit not essential; if
camping off-site ask permission wherever
possible*
can¹: una lata
  a can of beer una lata de cerveza [l*a*h-tadeh
  therv*e*h-tha]
  can-opener un abrelatas [ah-brehl*a*h-tas]
can²: can I have . . . ? ¿me da . . . ? [meh da]
  can you show me . . . ? ¿podría
  enseñarme . . . ? [pod-r*ee*-a ensen-y*a*r-meh]
  I can't . . . no puedo [noh pw*e*h-doh]
  I can't swim no sé nad*a*r [. . . seh . . .]
  he can't . . . no puede [noh pw*e*h-deh]
  we can't . . . no podemos [noh pod-*e*h-moss]
Canada Canad*á*
Canadian canadiense [−yen-seh]
cancel anul*a*r
  I want to cancel my reservation quiero
  anular mi reserva [kee-*e*h-roh anool*a*r mee reh-
  s*a*irva]

can we cancel dinner for tonight?
¿podríamos no cenar aquí esta noche?
[podr*ee*-amoss no theh-n*a*r ak*ee* . . .]
candle una vela [veh-la]
   by candlelight a la luz de una vela
   [. . . looth . . .]
cane un bastón
capsize volcarse [vol-k*a*r-seh]
car un coche [k*o*h-cheh]
carafe una garrafa
carbonated con gas
carburetor el carburador [−boo−]
cards las cartas
   do you play cards? ¿juega usted a las cartas?
   [*h*weh-ga oost*e*h . . .]
care: good-bye, take care adiós, cuídese
   [kw*ee*deh-seh]
   will you take care of this for me? ¿puede
   usted guardarme esto? [pw*e*h-deh oost*e*h
   gwar-d*a*r-meh *e*sstoh]
careful: be careful tenga cuidado
   [. . . kwee-d*a*h-doh]
car ferry un ferry
carpet la alfombra
carrot una zanahoria [thanna-*o*ree-a]
carry llev*a*r
   could you carry this for me? ¿podría usted
   llevarme esto? [pod-r*ee*-a oost*e*h yeh-v*a*r-meh
   *e*sstoh]
carving una talla [t*a*-ya]
case *(suitcase)* la maleta [mall*e*h-tah]
cash dinero [dee-n*e*h-roh]
   I haven't any cash no tengo dinero en
   efectivo [. . . effekt*ee*-voh]
   I'll pay cash voy a pag*a*r al contado
   cash register la caja [k*a*h-*h*a]
   will you cash a check for me? ¿podría
   hacerme efectivo un cheque? [pod-r*ee*-a
   ath*ai*r-meh effekt*ee*-voh oon cheh-keh]
casino el casino
cassette una cassette

castle el castillo [kass-*tee*-yoh]
cat un gato
catch: where do we catch the bus? ¿dónde se
coge el autobús? [don-deh seh k*o*-*h*eh el
ow-toh-b*oo*ss]
   he's caught a bug ha cogido una infección
   [ah ko-*h*eedoh *oo*na eem-fekth-yon]
cathedral la catedr*a*l
Catholic católico
cauliflower una coliflor
cave una cueva [kweh-va]
ceiling el techo
celery apio [*a*h-pee-oh]
centigrade centígrado [then-*tee*-gra-doh]
» *TRAVEL TIP: to convert C to F:* $\frac{C}{5} \times 9 + 32 = F$

   centigrade −5 0 10 15 21 30 36.9
   Fahrenheit 23 32 50 59 70 86 98.4
centimeter un centímetro [then-t*ee*−]
» *TRAVEL TIP: 1 cm = 0.39 inches*
central central [thentr*a*l]
   with central heating con calefacción central
   [. . . kalleh-fakth-yon . . .]
center el centro [th−]
centro ciudad *city center*
cerrado *closed*
certain cierto [thee-*a*ir-toh]
   are you certain? ¿está usted seguro? [est*a*
   *oo*st*e*h seh-g*oo*-roh]
certificate un certificado [th−]
   birth certificate partida de nacimiento
   [. . . nathee-mee-*e*ntoh]
chain una cadena [ka-d*e*h-na]
chair una silla [*see*-ya]
   chairlift telesilla [teleh−]
champagne champ*á*n
**change: could you change this into
pesetas?** ¿puede cambiarme esto en pesetas?
[pweh-dah kam-bee-*a*r-meh . . .]
   I don't have any change no tengo nada
   suelto [. . . sw*e*ll-toh]

do we have to change trains? ¿tenemos que cambiar de tren? [teh-neh-moss keh . . .]
I'll just get changed me voy a cambiar
» *TRAVEL TIP: changing money; look for "cambio" sign; write checks in English; take your passport*
channel: the Channel el Canal de la Mancha
charge: what will you charge? ¿cuánto me va a cobrar? [kwanto meh . . .]
   who's in charge? ¿quién está a cargo de esto? [kee-*en* . . .]
chart *(sea)* carta de navegación [. . . deh na-veh-gath-yon]
cheap barato
   have you got something cheaper? ¿tiene alguna otra cosa más barata? [tee-eh-neh . . .]
cheat: I've been cheated me han engañado [meh an engan-yah-doh]
check: un cheque [cheh-keh]
   will you take a check? ¿aceptan cheques? [athep-tan . . .]
   checkbook talonario de cheques [talon-ar-yo . . .]
   traveler's check un cheque de viaje [cheh-keh deh vee-ah-heh]
» *TRAVEL TIP: see* **change**
   will you check? ¿quiere asegurarse? [kee-eh-reh asseh-goorar-seh]
   I'm sure, I've checked estoy seguro, lo he comprobado [loh eh . . .]
   will you check the total? ¿quiere repasar la suma? [kee-eh-reh . . .]
   we checked in nos inscribimos [eenskreebeemoss]
   we checked out dejamos el hotel [deh-ha-moss . . .]
cheek la mejilla [meh-hee-ya]
cheers *(toast)* salud [saloo]
cheese queso [keh-soh]
   cheesecake tarta de queso
   say cheese sonría [son-ree-a]
chef el jefe de cocina [heh-feh deh ko-thee-na]

chest el pecho
» *TRAVEL TIP: chest measurements*

US	34	36	38	40	42	44	46
Spain	87	91	97	102	107	112	117

chickenpox varicela [varee-theh-la]
child un niño [neen-yoh]
  children los niños
  children's portions medias porciones para
  niños [mehd-yass porth-yoness . . .]
» *TRAVEL TIP: children are welcome almost
  everywhere as family life is very strong in
  Spain*
chin la barbilla [bar-bee-ya]
china porcelana [por-theh-lah-na]
chips *(casino)* fichas [feechass]
chocolate chocolate [−lah-teh]
  a box of chocolates una caja de bombones
  [kah-ha]
  hot chocolate chocolate a la taza [tah-tha]
choke *(car)* el aire [eye-reh]
chop *(noun)* una chuleta [choo−]
  pork/lamp chop una chuleta de cerdo/de
  cordero [. . . thair-doh . . .]
Christmas Navidad
  Merry Christmas Feliz Navidad [feleeth . . .]
» *TRAVEL TIP: Spaniards celebrate Christmas Eve,
  New Year's Eve and the 6th of January, when
  presents are given*
church una iglesia [ee-gleh-see-a]
  **where is the Protestant/Catholic
  Church?** ¿dónde está la iglesia protestante/
  católica?
cider sidra [seedra]
cigar un puro [poo-roh]
cigarette un cigarillo [theegaree-yo]
  would you like a cigarette? ¿quiere un
  cigarillo? [kee-eh-reh . . .]
  filtered/plain cigarettes . . . con filtro/sin
  filtro
» *TRAVEL TIP: if you prefer mild tobacco ask for
  "tabaco rubio"* [. . . roob-yo]

circle un círculo [th*ee*rkooloh]
city una ciudad [thee-oo-d*a*]
claim *(insurance)* una reclamación [–ath-yon]
clarify aclar*a*r
clean *(adjective)* limpio [l*ee*mp-yo]
   can I have some clean sheets? ¿quiere
   ponerme sábanas l*i*mpias? [kee-*e*h-reh
   pon-*ai*rmeh . . .]
   my room hasn't been cleaned today hoy no
   han limpiado mi habitación [*o*y no an
   leemp-y*a*h-doh mee abbee-tath-yon]
   it's not clean no est*á* limpio
clear: I'm not clear about it no lo comprendo
   bien [. . . bee-*e*n]
   clear up: do you think it'll clear up
   later? ¿cree usted que se despejará?
   [kr*e*h-eh . . . keh seh desspeh-h*a*ra]
clever listo [l*ee*-stoh]
climate el clima [kl*ee*ma]
clip *(ski)* un gancho
clock el reloj [reh-l*o*h]
close cerca [th*ai*r-ka]
close: when do you close? ¿a qué hora se
   cierra? [ah keh *o*ra seh thee-*e*rra]
closed cerrado [th–]
cloth tela; *(rag)* un trapo
clothes la ropa
cloud una nube [n*oo*beh]
clutch *(car)* el embrague [embr*a*-gheh]
   the clutch is slipping patina el embrague
coast la costa
   coast guard un guardacostas [gwa–]
coat un abrigo [–br*ee*–]
coatroom el guardarropa [gwa–]
coche-restaurante *dining car*
cockroach una cucaracha
coffee café
   coffee with milk/black coffee café con
   leche/café solo [. . . kon l*e*h-cheh . . .]
coin una moneda [mon*e*h-da]
cold frío [fr*ee*-oh]

I'm cold tengo frío
I've got a cold tengo un resfriado
collapse: he's collapsed ha sufrido un colapso
[ah soofr*ee*doh]
collar el cuello [kw*eh*-yo]
» *TRAVEL TIP: collar sizes*

US:	14	14½	15	15½	16	16½	17
Spanish:	36	37	38	39	41	42	43

collar bone la clavícula [−*ee*koo−]
collect: I want to collect... quería recoger...
[keh-*ree*-a reh-ko*h*air]
color color
have you any other colors? ¿lo tiene en
otros colores? [... tee-*eh*-neh...]
comb un peine [p*ay*-neh]
come venir [ven*ee*r]
I come from London soy de Londres
we came here yesterday llegamos ayer
[yeh-g*a*moss ah-y*air*]
come on! ¡vamos! [b*a*h-moss]
come with me venga conmigo
[... kon-m*ee*goh]
comedor dining room
comfortable cómodo
it's not very comfortable no es muy cómodo
[... mwee...]
Common Market el Mercado Común
[mair-k*a*h-doh komm*oo*n]
company compañía [kompan-y*ee*-ah]
you're good company es usted una
compañía agradable
[... oost*eh*... agrad*a*h-bleh]
compartment *(train)* un compartimento
compass una brújula [br*oo-h*oo-la]
compensation una indemnización
[−thath-y*on*]
I demand compensation exijo una
indemnización [eggs-*ee*h*oh*...]
complain quejarse [keh-*h*arseh]
I want to complain about my room/the
waiter quiero present*ar* una queja sobre mi

....

habitación/el camarero [kee-*e*h-ro ... keh-*h*a
s*o*h-breh mee abbee-tath-y*o*n]
have you got a complaints book? ¿tiene
usted un libro de reclamaciones? [tee-*e*h-neh
oost*e*h oon l*ee*broh deh reklamath-yoness]
completely completamente [−teh]
completo no vacancies
complicated: it's very complicated es muy
complicado [... mwee ...]
**compliment: my compliments to the
chef** felicite al jefe de cocina de mi parte
[feleeth*e*eteh al *h*eh-feh deh ko-th*ee*na deh mee
p*a*rteh]
concert un concierto [kon-thee-*ai*r-toh]
concussion una conmoción cerebral
[konmoth-y*o*n thereh-br*a*l]
condition la condición [kondeeth-y*o*n]
it's not in very good condition no est*á* en
muy buenas condiciones [... mw*ee* bweh-nass
kon-deeth-yoness]
condom un cond*ó*n
conference un congreso
confession una confesión [konfess-y*o*n]
confirm confirmar [konfeerm*a*r]
confuse: you're confusing me me deja usted
hecho un lío [meh d*e*h-*h*a oost*e*h *e*h-cho oon
l*ee*-oh]
congratulations! ¡enhorabuena! [enora-bw*e*h-na]
conjunctivitis conjunctivitis
[kon-*h*oonteev*e*eteess]
connection *(travel)* el enlace [en-l*a*h-theh]
connoisseur un experto [−p*ai*r−]
conscious consciente [kons-thee-*e*nteh]
consciousness: he's lost consciousness ha
perdido el conocimiento [ah pa*i*rd*e*edoh el
konotheem-y*e*ntoh]
conserje concierge
consigna left luggage
constipation estreñimiento
[esstren-yeem-y*e*ntoh]
consul el c*ó*nsul

consulate el consulado
contact: how can I contact...? ¿cómo puedo ponerme en contacto con...? [... pweh-doh pon-airmeh...]
  contact lenses lentes de contacto [lentess...]
contraceptive un anticonceptivo [−thepteevoh]
convenient conveniente [konven-yenteh]
cook: it's not cooked no está cocido [ko-thee-doh]
  it's beautifully cooked está guisado maravillosamente [... ghee-sah-doh maravee-yosa-menteh]
  you're a good cook es usted un buen cocinero [ess oosteh oon bwen kotheeneh-roh]
cool fresco
corkscrew un sacacorchos
corn *(foot)* un callo [ka-yoh]
corner: on the corner en la esquina [ess-keena]
  in the corner en el rincón
  can we have a corner table? ¿puede darnos una mesa cerca de un rincón? [pweh-deh... meh-sa thair-ka...]
cornflakes copos de maíz [... mah-eeth]
correct correcto
cosmetics cosméticos
cost: what does it cost? ¿cuánto cuesta? [kwantoh kwessta]
  that's too much es demasiado caro [demass-yah-doh]
  I'll take it me lo llevo [meh loh yeh-voh]
cotton algodón
cough *(noun)* tos [toss]
  cough drops pastillas para la tos [pass-teeyass...]
  cough medicine una medicina para la tos [meddee-theena...]
could: could you please...? ¿podría usted...? [podree-a oosteh...]
  could I have...? quiero... [kee-eh-roh]
country país [pa-eess]
  in the country en el campo

couple: a couple of... un par de...
courier el guía turístico [ghee-a...]
course *(of meal)* un plato
  of course por supuesto [...soopwestoh]
court: I'll take you to court voy a demandarle
  a usted [boy ah deh-mandar-leh ah oosteh]
cousin: my cousin mi primo [...pree−]
cover: keep him covered manténgale abrigado
  [−ga-leh...]
  cover charge el precio del cubierto [preth-yo
  del koob-yairtoh]
cow una vaca
crab un cangrejo [kangreh-hoh]
craft shop una tienda de artesanía [tee-enda
  deh artessanee-a]
crash: there's been a crash ha habido un
  accidente [ah abeedoh oon ak-theedenteh]
  crash helmet un casco
crazy loco
  you're crazy está usted loco [...oosteh...]
cream crema [kreh-ma]
crèche una guardería infantil
  [gwar-deh-ree-a...]
credit card una tarjeta de crédito
  [tar-heh-ta...]
crisis crisis [kree-seess]
crossroads un cruce [kroo-theh]
crowded atestado
cruce crossroads
cruise un crucero [krootheh-roh]
crutch una muleta [moo−]
cry llorar [yorrar]
  don't cry no llore [noh yo-reh]
cup una taza [tatha]
  a cup of coffee un café
cupboard un armario [armar-yoh]
currency exchange cambio
curry "curry" [koo−]
curtains las cortinas
cushion un cojín [ko-heen]
Customs la aduana [ad-wah-na]

cut: I've cut myself me he cortado [meh eh . . .]
cycle: can we cycle there? ¿se puede ir en
  bicicleta? [seh pweh-deh eer en beetheekleh-ta]
cyclist un ciclista [theekl*ee*sta]
cylinder el cilindro [theel*ee*endroh]
  cylinder-head gasket la junta de culata
  [h*oo*nta deh kool*ah*-ta]
dad(dy) papá
damage: I'll pay for the damage pagaré los
  desperfectos [−r*eh* . . .]
  it's damaged es defectuoso [−too-*o*soh]
damas ladies
damn! ¡maldita sea! [mal-d*ee*-ta s*eh*-a]
damp húmedo [*oo*meh-doh]
dance: is there a dance on? ¿va a haber baile?
  [ba ab*air* bye-leh]
  would you like to dance? ¿bailas conmigo?
  [bye-lass konm*ee*goh]
dangerous peligroso
dark oscuro [−k*oo*−]
  dark blue azul oscuro [ath*oo*l . . .]
  when does it get dark? ¿a qué hora
  oscurece? [ah keh *o*ra oss-koor*eh*-theh]
darling querido [keh-r*ee*doh]
  (to woman) querida
dashboard el cuadro [kw*a*−]
date: what's the date? ¿qué fecha es hoy?
  [keh . . .]
  it's the eighteenth of June es el dieciocho de
  junio [. . . dee-ethee-*o*tcho deh *hoo*n-yoh]
  in 1982 en mil novecientos ochenta y dos
  [meel noveh-thee-*e*ntoss otch*e*nt-eye-d*o*ss]
  can we make a date? ¿podemos citarnos?
  [pod*eh*-moss theet*a*r-noss]
  dates *(fruit)* dátiles [d*ah*-teeless]
» *TRAVEL TIP: to say the date in Spanish you just
  use the ordinary number (see pages 124–125),
  the exception being:* **the first** el primero
daughter: my daughter mi hija [mee *ee*-h*a*]
day el día [d*ee*-a]

the day after el día de después
[. . . dess-pwess]
the day before el día de antes [. . . antess]
dead muerto [moo-airtoh]
deaf sordo
  hearing-aid un aparato del oído [o-eedoh]
deal un negocio [negoth-yoh]
  it's a deal trato hecho [. . . etchoh]
  will you deal with it? ¿puede usted ocuparse
  de ello? [pweh-deh oosteh okkoopar-seh
  deheh-yoh]
dear: Dear Sir muy señor mío
  Dear Madam estimada señora
  Dear Francisco querido Francisco
  (written by a man) mi querido amigo
December diciembre [deeth-yembreh]
deck la cubierta [koob-yairta]
  deckchair una tumbona [toom—]
declare: I have nothing to declare no tengo
  nada que declarar [. . . keh . . .]
deep profundo
  is it deep? ¿es muy profundo? [. . . mwee . . .]
defendant el acusado [—koo—]
delay: the flight was delayed el vuelo se
  retrasó [vweh-loh seh reh—]
deliberately a propósito
delicate *(health)* delicado
delicatessen "delicatessen"
delicious delicioso [deleeth-yosoh]
delivery el reparto [reh—]
  is there another mail delivery? ¿hay otro
  reparto de correo? [eye . . . korreh-oh]
deluxe de lujo [deh loo-hoh]
democratic democrático
demonstration *(of gadget, etc.)* una
  demostración [—ath-yon]
dent una abolladura [aboya-doora]
  you've dented my car me ha abollado usted
  el coche [meh ah aboyyah-doh oosteh el
  kotcheh]

dentist un dentista
  YOU MAY HEAR...
  abra todo lo que pueda—*open wide*
  enjuáguese [en-*h*wah-gheh-seh]—*rinse out*
dentures dentadura postiza [... poss-t*ee*tha]
deny: I deny it lo niego [... nee-eh-goh]
deodorant un desodor*a*nte [−teh]
departure la salida [−*ee*da]
depend: it depends (on ...) depende (de)...
  [deh-p*e*ndeh deh]
deport deport*a*r [deh−]
deposit un depósito [deh−]
  do I have to leave a deposit? ¿hay que dejar
  un depósito? [eye keh de*h*ar ...]
depressed deprimido
depth profundidad
despacho de billetes *ticket office*
desperate: I'm desperate for a drink me
  muero por una copa [meh mweh-roh ...]
dessert el postre [p*o*ss-treh]
destination dest*i*no
detergent un detergente [detair-*h*enteh]
desvío *diversion*
detour un rodeo [rod*e*h-oh]
devalued devaluado [−w*a*-doh]
develop: could you develop these? ¿podría
  revel*a*rmelas? [podr*ee*-a reh-vel*a*r-meh-lass]
diabetic diab*é*tico
diamond un diamante [dee-ah-m*a*nteh]
diaper un pañal [pan-y*a*]
diarrhea diarrea [dee-arr*e*h-a]
  have you got something for diarrhea?
  ¿tiene usted algo para la diarrea? [tee-*e*h-neh
  ost*e*h ...]
diary una agenda [ah-*h*enda]
dictionary un diccionario [deekth-yon*a*r-yoh]
die morir [mor*ee*r]; **he's dying** se est*á* muriendo
  [seh ... moor-yendoh]
didn't *see* **not**
diesel *(fuel)* gas-oil

....

diet dieta [dee-*eh*-ta]
  I'm on a diet est*oy* a dieta
different: they are different son dif*erentes*
  can I have a different room? quisiera otra
  habitación distinta [keess-yeh-ra otra
  abbee-tath-yon...]
difficult difícil [deef*eet*heel]
digestion la digestión [dee-*h*est-yon]
dinghy una barquita [−k*ee*−]
dining car *(on train)* vagón restaurante
  [...rest-ow-r*a*nteh]
dining room el comedor [kommeh-d*o*r]
dinner la cena [theh-na]
  (lunch) el almuerzo [almw*ai*r-thoh]
dinner jacket un smoking
» *TRAVEL TIP: dinner normally available 9-11 pm*
dipped headlights luces cortas [l*oo*thess...]
dirección única one-way *(street)*
direct *(adjective)* directo [dee−]
  does it go direct? ¿va directo?
dirty sucio [s*oo*th-yoh]
disabled minusválido [mee-nooss−]
disappear desaparecer [−eth*ai*r]
  it's just disappeared se ha debido esfumar
  [seh ah deb*ee*doh ess-foom*a*r]
disappointing decepcionante
  [deth-epth-yon*a*nteh]
disco una discot*e*ca; **see you in the disco** te
  veré en la discoteca [teh veh-r*eh*...]
discount una rebaja [reb*a*h-ha]
disgusting asquer*o*so [asskeh−]
dish un plato
dishonest poco honrado [...on−]
disinfectant un desinfect*a*nte [−teh]
distance la distancia [−thee-a]
  in the distance a lo lejos [...leh-*h*oss]
distilled water agua destil*a*da [*a*hg-wa...]
distress signal una llamada de socorro
  [yam*a*h-da...]
distributor *(car)* el distribuidor [−weed*o*r]

disturb: the noise is disturbing us nos está
  molestando el ruido [. . . roo-*ee*doh]
divorced divorciado [deevorth-y*a*do]
do: how do you do? hola, ¿qué tal? [oh-la
  keh . . .]
  what are you doing tonight? ¿qué vas a
  hacer esta noche? [keh vass ath*air* . . .]
  how do you do it? ¿cómo se hace? [. . . seh
  *a*h-theh]
  will you do it for me? ¿me lo quiere hacer
  usted? [. . . kee-*e*h-reh ath*air* oost*e*h]
  I've never done it before no lo he hecho en
  mi vida [. . . eh *e*h-tchoh . . .]
  he did it lo hizo [lo *ee*-thoh]
  I was doing 60 kph iba a sesenta kilómetros
  por hora [*ee*ba ah . . . *o*ra]
doctor el médico
  I need a doctor necesito un médico
  [nethess*ee*toh . . .]
  YOU MAY HEAR . . .
  ¿ha tenido esto antes? [ah teneedoh . . .] *have*
  you had this before?
  ¿dónde le duele? [dondeh leh dweh-leh] *where*
  does it hurt?
  ¿está tomando algún medicamento? *are you*
  taking any drugs?
  tómese una/dos de estas cada tres horas/al
  día/dos veces al día *take one/two of these every*
  three hours/every day/twice a day
document un documento [−koo−]
dog un perro
don't! ¡no lo haga! [. . . *a*h-ga] *see* **not**
door una puerta [pw*air*-ta]
dosage una dosis [d*o*h-seess]
double: double room una habitación doble
  [abbee-tath-y*o*n d*o*h-bleh]
  double whisky un whisky doble
down: get down! ¡baje! [b*a*h-*h*eh]
  downstairs abajo [ab*a*h-*h*oh]
drain un sumidero [soo-mee-d*e*h-roh]

....

dress un vestido [−teed*oh*]

» *TRAVEL TIP: dress sizes*

US	5	7	9	11	12
Spain	38	38	40	40	42

dressing *(for wound)* vendaje [vend*ah*-*h*eh]
    (for salad) aliño [al*ee*n-yoh]

drink *(verb)* beber [beb*air*]
    (alcoholic) una copa
    would you like something to drink? ¿quiere
    usted beber algo? [kee-*eh*-reh oost*eh* . . .]
    I don't drink no bebo [. . . beh-boh]
    is the water drinkable? ¿es potable el agua?
    [ess pot*ah*-bleh el *ah*g-wa]
    I had too much to drink last night bebí
    demasiado anoche [beb*ee* demass-yah-doh
    an*o*tcheh]

drive: I've been driving all day llevo todo el
    día conduciendo [y*eh*-voh t*o*doh el d*ee*-a
    kondooth-yendoh]

driver el conducto*r* [−d*oo*k−]

driving license el permiso de conducir
    [pair-m*ee*-soh deh kondoo-th*ee*r]

» *TRAVEL TIP: driving in Spain; you will need
    registration documents and green card; seat
    belts compulsory out of town; red triangle and
    spare set of headlight bulbs legal requirements*

drown: he's drowning se está ahogando [seh
    esst*a* ah-o-gandoh]

drug un medicamento

drugstore una farmacia [far-m*ah*th-ya]

drunk borr*a*cho

dry seco [s*eh*-koh]

dry cleaning limpieza en seco [leemp-y*eth*a en
    s*eh*-koh]

ducha shower

due: when is the bus due? ¿a qué hora debe
    llegar el autobús? [ah keh *o*ra d*eh*-beh yeh-g*a*r
    el ow-tob*oo*ss]

during durante [doo-r*a*nteh]

dust polvo

duty-free el "duty-free"

dynamo la dinamo [deenah-moh]
each: can we have one each? ¿nos da uno a cada uno?
   how much are they each? ¿cuánto es cada uno? [kw– . . .]
ear la oreja [oreh-ha]
   I have an earache tengo dolor de oídos [. . . deh o-eedoss]
early temprano
   we want to leave a day earlier queremos irnos un día antes de lo previsto [keh-reh-moss eer-noss oon dee-a antess deh loh preh-veestoh]
earring un pendiente [–yenteh]
east este [essteh]
easy fácil [fah-theel]
Easter Semana Santa
eat comer [–air]
   something to eat algo de comer
egg un huevo [weh-voh]
eggplant una berenjena [berren-heh-na]
either: either . . . or . . . o . . . o . . .
   I don't like either no me gusta ninguno
elastic elástico
elbow el codo
electric eléctrico
   electric blanket una manta eléctrica
   electric heater una estufa eléctrica [esstoo-fa . . .]
electrical outlet una toma de corriente [. . . korr-yenteh]
electrician un electricista [–eethee–]
electricity electricidad [elektreetheeda]
elegant elegante [–teh]
elevator el ascensor
   the elevator isn't working no funciona el ascensor [noh foonth-yona el ass-thensor]
else: something else algo más
   somewhere else en otra parte [. . . –teh]
   let's go somewhere else vamos a otra parte
   who else? ¿quién más? [kee-en . . .]
   or else si no [see . . .]

embarrassing violento [vee–]
embarrassed avergonzado
[ah-vair-gon-th*a*h-doh]
embassy la embajada [emba*h*ada]
emergency una emergencia [em-air-*h*en-thee-ah]
empty vacío [–th*ee*–]
empuje *push*
encienda los faros *headlights on*
enclose: I enclose… adjunto… [–*h*oon–]
end el fin*a*l
  when does it end? ¿cuándo termina?
  [kw*a*ndoh tairm*ee*na]
engaged *(person)* prometido [–t*ee*–]
engagement ring el anillo de prometida
[an*ee*-yoh…]
engine el motor
  I've got engine trouble le pasa algo al motor
  [leh…]
England Inglaterra
English inglés [eengl*ess*]
  the English los ingleses [eengl*e*h-sess]
enjoy: I enjoyed it very much me gustó mucho
[meh goo-stoh m*oo*-choh]
enlargement *(photo)* una ampliación
[amplee-ath-yon]
enormous enorme [eh-n*o*r-meh]
enough suficiente [soo-f*ee*th-*y*enteh]
  thank you, that's enough gracias, es
  suficiente
entertainment diversiones [deevairs-yoh-ness]
entrada libre *admission free*
entrance la entr*a*da
entry la entr*a*da
envelope un sobre [s*o*h-breh]
equipment equipo [eh-k*ee*-poh]
error un error
escalator una escalera mecánica [ess-kal*e*h-ra
meh-k*a*nnika]
escuela *school*
especially especialmente [essp*e*th-yal-m*e*nteh]
espere *wait*

essential imprescindible
[eempress-theen-d*ee*bleh]
   it is essential that... es necesario que...
   [ess nethess*a*r-yoh keh]
estacionamiento limitado *restricted parking*
Europe Europa [eh-ooro*h*-pa]
evacuate desocupar [dessockoop*a*r]
even: even Americans hasta los américanos
   [*a*ssta...]
evening la tarde [t*a*r-deh]
   (after nightfall) la noche [n*o*tch-eh]
   good evening buenas tardes [bweh-nass t*a*rdess]
   this evening esta tarde/noche
   in the evening por la tarde
   evening dress traje de etiqueta [tra*h*-*h*eh deh
   ettee-k*e*h-ta]
   (woman's) traje de noche
ever: have you ever been to...? ¿ha estado
   alguna vez en...? [ah esst*a*h-doh al-g*oo*na
   veth en]
every cada
   every day todos los días [...dee-ass]
   everyone todos
   everything todo
   everywhere en todas partes [...p*a*rtess]
evidence pruebas [prweh-bass]
exact exacto [eggs-*a*ktoh]
example un ejemplo [e*h*em–]
   for example por ejemplo
excellent excelente [ess-thell*e*nteh]
except: except me menos yo [meh-noss...]
excess exceso [ess-th*e*h-soh]
   excess baggage exceso de equipaje [...deh
   eckee-p*a*heh]
exchange *(money)* cambio [k*a*m-bee-oh]
exciting emocionante [emoth-yon*a*nteh]
excursion una excursión [ess-koors-y*o*n]
excuse me *(to get past, etc.)* con permiso
   [...pair-m*ee*-soh]
   (to get attention) ¡por favor!
   (apology) perdone [pair-d*o*h-neh]

exhaust *(car)* el tubo de escape [*too*-boh deh
   ess-k*ah*-peh]
exhausted agot*a*do
exhibition una exposición [−seeth-y*o*n]
exhibitor el expositor [ess-possee-t*o*r]
exit la salida [−*lee*−]
expect: she's expecting est*á* esperando un niño
   [. . . n*ee*n-yoh]
expenses: it's on an expense account esto
   corre a cargo de la compañía
   [. . . korreh . . . kompan-y*ee*-a]
expensive caro
expert experto [essp*air*-toh]
explain explic*a*r
   would you explain that slowly? ¿podría
   explicar eso lentamente? [podr*ee*-a esspleek*a*r
   *e*h-so lenta-m*e*nteh]
export *(noun)* exportación [essportath-y*o*n]
express *(mail)* urgente [oor-*h*enteh]
extra: an extra glass otro vaso más
   [. . . v*ah*-soh . . .]
   is that extra? ¿eso es extra?
extremely extremadamente
   [esstreh-mah-d*a*menteh]
eye un ojo [*o*ho]
   eyebrow una ceja [th*e*h-*h*a]
   eye shadow sombra de ojos [*o*hoss]
   eyewitness un testigo presencial [tess*tee*goh
   pressenth-y*a*l]
face la cara
   face mask unas gafas de bucear [. . . deh
   booth*e*h-*a*r]
fact un hecho [*e*tcho]
factory una f*á*brica
Fahrenheit "Fahrenheit"
» *TRAVEL TIP: to convert F to C:* $F - 32 \times \frac{5}{9} = C$

Fahrenheit	23	32	50	59	70	86	98.4
centigrade	−5	0	10	15	21	30	36.9

faint: she's fainted se ha desmayado [seh ah
   dess-ma-y*ah*-doh]

fair *(fun-)* una verbena [vair-beh-na]
  (commercial) una feria [feh-ree-a]
  that's not fair no hay derecho [noh eye dereh-choh]
faithfully: yours faithfully le saluda atentamente
fake *(noun)* una falsificación [–ath-yon]
fall: he's fallen se ha caído [seh ah kah-ee-doh]
false falso [fal-soh]
  false teeth dientes postizos [dee-entess poss-tee-thoss]
family la familia [fameel-ya]
fan *(mechanical)* un ventilador
  (hand held) un abanico [–nee–]
  (football, etc.) un fan
  fan belt la correa del ventilador [korreh-ah . . .]
far lejos [leh-hoss]
  is it far? ¿está lejos?
  how far is it? ¿a qué distancia está [ah keh dee-stanth-ya . . .]
fare *(travel)* el billete [bee-yeh-teh]
farm una granja [gran-ha]
farther más allá [mass a-yah]
fashion la moda
fast rápido
  don't speak so fast no hable tan de prisa [noh ah-bleh tan deh pree-sa]
fat *(adjective)* gordo
  (on meat) grasa
fatal mortal
father: my father mi padre [mee pah-dreh]
fathom una braza [–th–]
faucet el grifo [greefoh]
fault *(defect)* un defecto
  it's not my fault no es culpa mía [koolpa mee-a]
faulty defectuoso [deh-fekt-woh-soh]
favorite favorito [fah-voree-toh]
February febrero [feh-breh-roh]
fed up: I'm fed up ¡estoy harto! [ar-toh]

....

feel sentir [−*teer*]
  I feel hot/cold tengo calor/frío [fr*ee*-oh]
  I feel sad estoy triste [tr*ee*ss-teh]
  I feel like... tengo ganas de... [...deh]
ferry el ferry
fever fiebre [fee-*e*h-breh]
  he's got a fever tiene fiebre [tee-*e*h-neh
  fee-*e*h-breh]
few: only a few solo unos pocos
  a few days unos días [...d*ee*−]
fiancé: my fiancé mi novio [mee n*o*h-vee-oh]
fiancée: my fiancée mi novia
field un campo
fifty-fifty a medias [ah m*e*h-dee-ass]
figs higos [*ee*-goss]
figure una figura [−g*oo*−]
  (number) cifra [th*ee*−]
  I'm watching my figure estoy cuidando la
  línea [...kweed*a*ndoh la l*ee*neh-a]
fill: fill her up llénelo [yeh-neh-loh]
  to fill in a form rellenar un impreso
  [reh-yeh-n*a*r oon eempr*e*h-soh]
fillet un filete [fee-leh-teh]
film una película [peh-l*ee*-koola]
  do you have this type of film? ¿tiene
  películas de este tipo? [tee-*e*h-neh
  peh-l*ee*-koolass deh *e*ss-teh t*ee*-poh]
filter filtro [f*ee*l−]; **filter or non-filter?** ¿con o
  sin filtro? [...seen...]
final de autopista end of freeway
find encontr*a*r
  if you find it... si lo encuentra... [see loh
  enkw*e*ntra]
  I've found a... he encontrado un... [eh...]
fine *(weather)* bueno [bw*e*h-noh]
  a 3,000 peseta fine una multa de tres mil
  pesetas [...meel peh-s*e*h-tass]
  OK, that's fine vale, muy bien [b*a*h-leh, mw*ee*
  bee-*e*n]
finger un dedo [d*e*h-doh]
  fingernail una uña [*oo*n-ya]

finish: I haven't finished no he terminado [no eh tairmeen*a*h-doh]

fire: fire! ¡fuego! [fw*e*h-goh]

    can we light a fire here? ¿se puede encender fuego aquí? [seh pw*e*h-deh enthen-d*ai*r fw*e*h-goh ak*ee*]

    fire department los bomberos [bomb*e*h-ross]

    fire extinguisher un extintor [ess-teen-t*o*r]

» TRAVEL TIP: *number for fire department will be in front of phone directory*

firme deslizante slippery surface

first el primero [pree-m*e*h-roh]

    I was first yo soy el primero

    first aid primeros auxilios [pree-m*e*h-ross ah-ook-s*ee*l-yoss]

    first aid kit un botiquín [−k*ee*n]

    first class primera clase [. . . −seh]

    first name nombre de pila [n*o*mbreh deh p*ee*la]

fish un pez [peth]; *(food)* pescado

fishing la pesca

    fishing rod una caña de pescar [kan-ya deh . . .]

    fishing tackle un aparejo de pesca [apar*e*h-*h*oh deh . . .]

fix: can you fix it? *(arrange, repair)* ¿lo puede arreglar? [pweh-deh . . .]

flag una bandera [−d*e*h−]

flash *(photo)* flash

flat llano [y*a*h-noh]

    this drink is flat esta bebida está floja [. . . flo-*h*a]

    I've got a flat (tire) tengo una (rueda) deshinchada [. . . rw*e*h-da dess eench*a*h-da]

flavor sabor

flea una pulga [p*oo*−]

flight vuelo [vw*e*h-loh]

flippers aletas

flirt *(verb)* coquetear [kockeh-teh-*a*r]

float *(verb)* flot*a*r

floor el suelo [sw*e*h-loh]

on the second floor en el segundo piso
[. . . pee-soh]
» TRAVEL TIP: *Europeans call the second floor the first floor, the third floor the second floor, etc.*
flower una flor
bunch of flowers un ramo de flores [–floress]
flu gripe [gree-peh]
fly *(insect)* una mosca
(on trousers) la bragueta [–gheh–]
foggy: it's foggy hay niebla [eye nee-eh-bla]
follow seguir [–gheer]
food comida [kommeeda]
food poisoning intoxicación alimenticia
[intoxicath-yon aleementeeth-ya]
fool tonto
foot un pie [pee-eh]
» TRAVEL TIP: *1 foot = 30.1 cm = 0.3 meters*
for para
forbidden prohibido [pro-eebee-doh]
foreign extranjero [–heh-roh]
foreign exchange divisas [dee-vee-sass]
foreigner un extranjero [–heh-roh]
forest un bosque [boss-keh]
forget olvidar [olvee-dar]
I forget, I've forgotten no me acuerdo, me he
olvidado [noh meh ak-wair-doh, meh eh . . .]
don't forget no se olvide [. . . –vee-deh]
I'll never forget you nunca te olvidaré
[. . . teh olvee-dareh]
fork un tenedor
form *(document)* hoja [oh-ha]
formal formal
(person) estirado [–tee–]
(dress) de etiqueta [–eekeh–]
fortnight quince días [keen-theh dee-ass]
forward hacia adelante [ath-ya . . . –teh]
could you forward my mail? ¿puede
enviarme el correo a mi nueva dirección?
[pweh-deh embee-armeh el korreh-oh ah mee
nweh-va deerek-thee-on]
forwarding address nueva dirección

foundation *(makeup)* crema base [kreh-ma bah-seh]
fracture una fractura
fragile frágil [frah-heel]
France Francia [franth-ya]
fraud un fraude [fra-oo-deh]
free libre [lee-breh]
   admission free entrada gratis
freeway autopista [ow-topeesta]
freight mercancías [–theeass]
French francés [–thess]
French fries patatas fritas [. . . freetass]
freshen up: I want to freshen up quiero refrescarme [kee-eh-roh reh-freskar-meh]
Friday viernes [vee-air-ness]
fried egg un huevo frito [weh-voh free-toh]
friend un amigo [amee-goh]
friendly simpático
from de [deh]
   where is it from? ¿de dónde es?
front *(noun)* la parte delantera [parteh delanteh-ra]; **in front of you** delante de usted [delan-teh deh oosteh]; **at the front** por delante
frost escarcha
   frostbite congelación [kon-heh-lath-yon]
frozen congelado [kon-heh–]
fruit fruta [froo–]
fruit salad macedonia de frutas [mathedon-ya deh . . .]
fry freír [freh-eer]
   nothing fried nada frito [free–]
   frying pan una sartén
full lleno [yeh–]
fun: it's fun es divertido [deev-air-teedoh]
funny *(strange)* raro
   (comical) gracioso [grath-yoh-soh]
furniture muebles [mweh-bless]
further más allá [. . . a-yah]
fuse el fusible [foo-see-bleh]

....

future futuro [foot*oo*-roh]
  in the future en lo sucesivo [soo-thess-*ee*voh]
gale un vendav*a*l
gallon un gal*ó*n
» *TRAVEL TIP: 1 gallon = 3.8 liters*
gallstone un cálculo biliario [k*a*lkooloh
  beel-y*a*ree-oh]
gamble jug*a*r [*h*oo–]
garage *(repair)* un taller [ta-y*a*ir]
  (parking) un garage [gar*a*-*h*eh]
garbage basura [–s*oo*–]
garden el jardín [*h*ard*ee*n]
garlic ajo [*a*h-ho]
gas gas, gasolina [–l*ee*–]
  gas cylinder una bombona de gas
  gas pedal el acelerador [atheh-ler*a*dor]
  gas station una gasolinera [–eeneh-ra]
» *TRAVEL TIP: gas stations rarely have a
  mechanic–if in trouble try nearest "taller"*
gasket una junta [*h*oo–]
gay *(homosexual)* "gay" [guy]
gear *(car)* marcha
  (equipment) equipo [–k*ee*–]
  I have gearbox trouble le pasa algo a la caja
  de cambios [leh ... k*a*h-*h*a deh k*a*mb-yoss]
  gearshift la palanca de velocidades
  [... velothee-d*a*h-dess]
  I can't get it into gear no le entra la marcha
gesture un gesto [*he*–]
get: will you come and get me? ¿quiere venir a
  buscarme? [kee-*e*h-reh ven*ee*r ah boosk*a*r-meh]
  will you get me a ...? ¿me quiere busc*a*r
  un ...? [kee-*e*h-reh ...]
  how do I get to ...? ¿cómo se va a ... ?
  when can I get it back? ¿cuándo puedo
  recogerlo? [... pweh-doh reh-koh-*h*air-loh]
  where do I get off? ¿dónde tengo que
  bajarme? [... ba*h*armeh]
  when do we get back? ¿a qué hora
  volvemos? [ah keh *o*ra ...]

where can I get a bus for . . . ? ¿dónde se
coge el autobús para . . . ? [dondeh seh koh-heh
el ow-toh-booss . . .]
have you got . . . ? ¿tiene usted . . . ?
[tee-eh-neh oosteh]
gin ginebra [heeneh-bra]
  gin and tonic una tónica con ginebra
girl una chica [chee-ka]
  my girlfriend mi amiga [mee . . .]
give dar
  will you give me . . . ? ¿me quiere dar . . . ?
[meh kee-eh-reh . . .]
  I gave it to him se lo dí a él [. . . dee . . .]
glad alegre [–greh]
  I'm glad me alegro
gland una glándula [–doo–]
glass cristal; *(drinking)* un vaso
  a glass of water un vaso de agua [ahg-wa]
glasses *(eye)* las gafas
gloves guantes [gwantess]
glue cola
go ir [eer]
  when does the bus go? ¿a qué hora sale el
autobús [ah keh ora sah-leh el owtoh-booss]
  where are you going? ¿dónde va usted?
[dondeh va oosteh]
  let's go vámonos [bah-moh-noss]
  go on! ¡vamos! [b–]
  the bus has gone se nos ha ido el autobús
[. . . ah ee-doh . . .]
  he's gone se ha ido [seh . . .]
  my car won't go mi coche no anda
goat una cabra
  goat's cheese queso de cabra [keh-soh . . .]
God Dios [dee-oss]
goggles *(ski)* gafas de esquí [. . . esskee]
gold oro
golf el golf
good bueno [bweh-noh]
  good! ¡muy bien! [mwee bee-en]
good-bye adiós

gooseberries grosellas [groh-seh-yass]
gram un gramo
» *TRAVEL TIP: 100 grams = approx. 3½ oz.*
grand magnífico
  granddaughter nieta [nee-ehta]
  grandfather abuelo [abweh-loh]
  grandmother abuela
  grandson nieto [nee-ehtoh]
grapes uvas [oovass]
grapefruit pomelo [−meh−]
  grapefruit juice zumo de pomelo
  [thoomoh...]
grass hierba [yair-ba]
grateful agradecido [−dethee-doh]
  I'm very grateful to you se lo agradezco
  mucho [...agradeth-koh]
gratitude agradecimiento [−etheem-yentoh]
gravy salsa
gray gris [greess]
grease grasa
greasy grasiento [grass-yentoh]
great grande [−deh]
  great! ¡estupendo! [estoopendoh]
greedy codicioso [−eethee−]
  (for food) glotón
green verde [vair-deh]
greengrocer's la verdulería [vairdooleh-ree-a]
grocery la tienda de comestibles [tee-enda deh
komess-tee-bless]
ground el suelo [sweh-loh]
  on the ground en el suelo
  on the ground floor en la planta baja
  [...bah-ha]
group un grupo [groo−]
  our group leader el guía de nuestro grupo
  [ghee-a deh nwesstroh...]
  I'm with the North American group estoy
  en el grupo de los norteamericanos
guarantee la garantía [−tee-a]
  is there a guarantee? ¿tiene garantía?
  [tee-eh-neh...]

guest invitado [eembeet*ah*-doh]
guesthouse casa de huéspedes [k*ah*-sa deh
 w*e*sspedess]
guide un guía [gh*ee*-a]
guilty culpable [koolp*ah*-bleh]
guitar una guitarra [gheet*a*rra]
gum la encía [enth*ee*-a] *(chewing)* chicle
 [ch*ee*k-leh]
gun una pist*o*la
gynecologist un ginecólogo [*h*eeneh-k*o*llogoh]
hair el pelo [peh-loh]
 hairbrush un cepillo para el pelo
 [theh-p*ee*l-yoh . . .]
 bobby pin una horquilla [or-k*ee*-ya]
 where can I get a haircut? ¿dónde puedo
 cortarme el pelo? [d*o*n-deh pw*e*h-doh
 kort*a*r-meh . . .]
 is there a hairdresser's here? ¿hay alguna
 pelaquería aquí? [eye alg*oo*na pelookeh-r*ee*-ah
 ak*ee*]
half la mitad [la meet*ah*]
 a half portion media proción [m*a*id-ya
 porth-yon]
 half an hour media hora [m*a*id-ya *o*ra]
ham jamón de York [*h*amon . . .]
 hamburger una hamburguesa
 [amboor-gh*e*h-sa]
hammer un martillo [mart*ee*yoh]
hand una mano
 handbag un bolso
 handbrake el freno de mano
handkerchief un pañuelo [pan-yw*e*h-loh]
handle *(door)* el picaporte [–teh]
 (cup) el asa
hand luggage equipaje de mano
 [eck*ee*-p*ah*-*h*eh . . .]
handmade hecho a mano [*e*tcho . . .]
handsome guapo [gw*ah*-poh]
hanger una percha [p*ai*r-cha]
hangover resaca

my head is killing me parece que me va a estallar la cabeza [pareh-theh keh meh vah essta-yar la kabeh-tha]

happen suceder [sootheh-dair]

I don't know how it happened no sé cómo sucedió [. . . seh . . . soothehd-yoh]

what's happening/what's happened? ¿qué pasa/qué ha pasado? [keh ah . . .]

happy contento

harbor el puerto [pwair-toh]

hard duro [doo−]

(difficult) difícil [deefeetheel]

hard-boiled egg un huevo duro [weh-voh . . .]

push hard empuje fuerte [empoo-heh fwairteh]

harm *(noun)* daño [dahn-yoh]

hat sombrero

hate: I hate . . . detesto . . .

have tener [tenair]

I have no time no tengo tiempo [. . . tee-empoh]

do you have any cigars/a map? ¿tiene usted puros/un mapa? [tee-eh-neh oosteh . . .]

can I have some water/some more? ¿puede ponerme un poco de agua/un poco más? [pweh-deh poh-nair-meh . . .]

I have to leave tomorrow tengo que irme mañana [. . . keh eer-meh man-yah-na]

hay fever fiebre del heno [fee-eh-breh del eh-noh]

he él

does he live here? ¿vive aquí? [vee-veh akee]

he is my friend es amigo mío [. . . mee-oh]

he is ill está enfermo [−fair−]

head la cabeza [−tha]

headache dolor de cabeza

headlight un faro

head waiter el jefe de camareros [heh-feh deh kamareh-ross]

head wind viento contrario [vee-entoh kontrah-ree-oh]

health salud [sal*oo*]
  your health! ¡a tu salud! [ah too . . .]
healthy sano [s*a*h-noh]
hear: I can't hear no oigo [*oy*-goh]
  hearing aid un aparato del oído [o-*ee*doh]
heart el corazón [−thon]
  heart attack un infarto
heat calor
  heat stroke una insolación [−lath-y*o*n]
heater *(electric)* una estufa eléctrica
  [esst*oo*fa . . .]
heating calefacción [kaleh-fakth-y*o*n]
heavy pesado [peh-s*a*h-doh]
heel un tacón
  could you put new heels on these? ¿puede
  ponerles tapas nuevas? [pw*e*h-deh pon*air*-less
  t*a*pass nw*e*h-vass]
height altura [−*too*−]
hello! ¡hola! [*o*-la]
helmet un casco
help ayuda [−y*oo*−]
  can you help me? ¿puede ayudarme?
  [pw*e*h-deh ah-yoo-d*a*r-meh]
help! ¡socorro!
her: I know her la conozco [. . . kon*o*th-koh]
  will you give it to her? ¿quiere dárselo a
  ella? [kee-*e*h-reh d*a*rseh-loh a *e*h-ya]
  it's her es ella [ess *e*h-ya]
  it's her bag, it's hers es su bolso, es suyo
  [. . . s*oo*-yoh]
here aquí [ak*ee*]
  come here venga aquí [b*e*nga . . .]
high alto
highway autopista [ow-top*ee*sta]
hill un monte [−teh]
  up/down the hill cuesta arriba/abajo [kw*e*sta
  arr*ee*ba/ab*a*h-*h*oh]
him: I know him le conozco [leh kon*o*th-ko]
  will you give it to him? ¿quiere darselo a él?
  [kee-*e*h-reh . . .]
  it's him es él

his: it's his drink, it's his es su bebida, es suya [...*sooya*]
hit: he hit me me golpeó [golpeh-*oh*]
hitchhike hacer autostop [ath*air* owtoh-st*o*p]
  hitchhiker un autostopista [owto-stop*ee*sta]
hold *(verb)* tener [ten*air*]
hole un agujero [agoo-*h*eh-roh]
home casa [k*a*h-sa]
  I want to go home quiero irme a casa [kee-*e*h-roh *ee*r-meh...]
  at home en casa
  I'm homesick tengo morriña [morr*ee*n-ya]
honest honrado [on—]
  honestly? ¿de verdad? [deh vaird*a*]
honey miel [mee-*e*l]
honeymoon viaje de novios [vee-*a*h-*h*eh deh n*o*vee-oss]
hood *(car)* el capó
hope *(noun)* esperanza [—*a*ntha]
  I hope that... espero que... [essp*e*h-roh keh]
  I hope so/not espero que sí/no
horas de visita *visiting hours*
horizon el horizonte [oreeth*o*nteh]
horn *(car)* el claxon
horrible horrible [orr*ee*ebleh]
hors d'oeuvre entremeses [entreh-m*e*h-sess]
horse un caballo [—*a*-yoh]
hospital el hospital [ossp*ee*tal]
» *TRAVEL TIP: look for "Urgencias"—accident and emergency admissions; see also* **doctor**
host el anfitrión [amfeetree-*o*n]
hostess la anfitri*o*na
hot caliente [kal-y*e*nteh]
  (spiced) picante
hotel un hotel [oh-t*e*l]
hotplate la placa
hot-water bottle una bolsa de agua caliente [...*a*hg-wa kal-y*e*nteh]
hour una hora [*o*ra]
house una casa [k*a*h-sa]
  housewife ama de casa

how cómo
   how many cuántos [kw−]
   how much cuánto
   how often? ¿cada cuánto tiempo?
   [. . . tee-empoh]
   how long does it take? ¿cuánto se tarda?
   how long have you been here? ¿desde
   cuándo está usted aquí [dez-deh kwandoh esta
   oosteh akee]
   how are you? ¿como está usted? [. . . oosteh]
hull el casco
humid húmedo [oomeh-doh]
humor humor [oomor]
   you need a sense of humor hay que tener
   sentido del humor [eye keh tenair senteedoh
   del oomor]
hungry: I'm hungry/not hungry tengo/no
   tengo hambre [. . . ambreh]
hurry: I'm in a hurry tengo prisa [pree-sa]
   please hurry! ¡de prisa, por favor!
hurts: it hurts me duele [meh dweh-leh]
   my leg hurts me duele la pierna [pee-air-na]
   YOU MAY THEN HEAR . . .
   ¿es un dolor agudo? [. . . agoodoh] *is it a sharp
   pain?*
husband: my husband mi marido [mee
   mareedoh]
I yo
   I am a doctor/North American soy
   médico/norteamericano
   I am tired estoy cansado
   I live in New York vivo en Nueva York
   [vee-vo . . .]
ice hielo [yeh-loh]
   ice cream un helado [eh-lah-doh]
   iced coffee café helado
   with lots of ice con mucho hielo
identity papers los documentos de identidad
   [dokoomentoss deh eedentee-da]
idiot idiota [eed-yota]
if si [see]

ignition el encendido [enth-end*ee*-doh]
ill enfermo [−f*air*−]
  I feel ill me encuentro mal
  [...enk*went*roh...]
illegal ilegal [ee-leh-g*al*]
illegible ilegible [ee-leh-*hee*bleh]
illness una enfermedad [enfairmeh-d*a*]
immediately ahora mismo [ah-ora m*ee*zmoh]
import *(verb)* import*ar*
important import*a*nte [−teh]
  it's very important es muy importante
  [...mwee...]
import duty derechos de entrada
impossible imposible [−s*ee*bleh]
impressive impresionante [eempress-yon*a*nteh]
improve mejorar [me*hor*ar]
  I want to improve my Spanish quiero
  perfeccionar mi español [kee-*eh*-roh
  pairfekth-yon*ar* mee ess-pan-y*ol*]
in en
inch una pulgada
  » *TRAVEL TIP:* 1 *inch* = 2.54 *cm*
include incluír [een-klw*eer*]
  does that include breakfast? ¿está
  comprendido el desayuno? [est*a* comprend*ee*doh
  el dess-ay*oo*-noh]
inclusive inclusive [eenclos*ee*veh]
incompetent incompet*e*nte [−teh]
inconsiderate desconsider*a*do
incontinent incontin*e*nte [−teh]
incredible increíble [een-kreh-*ee*bleh]
indecent indecente [een-deh-th*e*nteh]
independent independiente [−y*e*nteh]
India India
Indian hindú [een-d*oo*]
indicator el indicad*o*r
indigestion una indigestión [eendee-*h*est-yon]
indoors en casa [k*a*h-sah]
industry la industria [eend*oo*stree-a]
infection una infección [eenfekth-yon]
infectious infeccioso [eenfekth-y*oh*-soh]

inflation inflación [eenflath-yon]
Información Information Office/Desk
informal informal
 (person) natural [–too–]
information información [–ath-yon–]
 **do you have any information in English
 about...?** ¿tiene alguna información en
 inglés sobre...? [tee-eh-neh algoona...
 soh-breh]
 is there an information office? ¿hay una
 oficina de información? [eye oona offee-theena
 deh...]
inhabitant un habitante [abeetanteh]
injection una inyección [een-yekth-yon]
injured herido [eh-ree-doh]
 he's been injured está herido
injury una herida [eh-ree-da]
innocent inocente [–thenteh]
insect un insecto
 insect repellent una loción
 ahuyentamosquitos [loth-yon ow-yenta–]
inside dentro de [...deh]
insist: I insist (on it) insisto (en ello) [...eh-yoh]
insomnia insomnio [een-somnee-oh]
instant coffee café instantáneo
 [eenstantah-neh-oh]
instead en cambio [kam-bee-oh]
 instead of... en lugar de... [en loogar deh]
insulating tape cinta aislante [theenta
 ah-eess-lanteh]
insulation aislamiento [ah-eeslam-yentoh]
insult un insulto [eensooltoh]
insurance el seguro [–goo–]
intelligent inteligente [eentellee-henteh]
interesting interesante [eenteh-reh-santeh]
international internacional [–nath-yonal]
interpret interpretar
 would you interpret for us? ¿podría usted
 hacer de intérprete nuestro? [podree-a oosteh
 ath-air deh eentair-preteh nwestroh]
into en

....

introduce: can I introduce ...? permítame
  presentarle a ... [pairmeeta-meh
  press-entar-leh ah]
invalid *(noun)* un inválido [eembalido]
invitation una invitación [eembeetath-yon]
  thank you for the invitation gracias por la
  invitación
invite invitar [eembeetar]
  can I invite you out? ¿te gustaría salir
  conmigo? [teh goostaree-a saleer konmeegoh]
invoice la factura [−too−]
Ireland Irlanda [eer−]
Irish irlandés [eerlandess]
iron *(noun: clothes)* una plancha
  will you iron these for me? ¿puede
  planchármelos? [pweh-deh planchar-meh-loss]
is es, está
island una isla [eess-la]
it lo
  it's not working no funciona
  [... foonth-yoh-na]
  give it to me démelo [deh-meh-loh]
  is it ...? es ...?, está ...?
itch picor
  it itches me pica [meh pee-ka]
itemize: would you itemize it for me? ¿me lo
  puede desglosar? [meh loh pweh-deh
  dez-gloh-sar]
jack el gato
jacket una chaqueta [chackeh-ta]
jam mermelada [mair-meh-lah-da]
  traffic jam un atasco
January enero [en-eh-roh]
jaw la mandíbula [−deeboo−]
jealous *(in love)* celoso [th−]
jeans unos vaqueros [vakeh-ross]
jellyfish una medusa [−doo−]
jetty el muelle [mweh-yeh]
jewelry joyas [hoy-yass]
jib el foque [foh-keh]
job un trabajo [−hoh−]

joke *(noun)* un chiste [ch*ee*ss-teh]
   you must be joking ¿pero lo dice en serio?
   [p*e*h-roh lo d*ee*theh en s*e*h-ree-oh]
journey un viaje [bee-*a*heh]
July julio [*hool*-yoh]
junction un cruce [kr*oo*-theh]
June junio [*hoo*n-yoh]
junk baratijas [barat*ee*-*h*ass]
just: just two sólo dos
   just a little sólo un poquito [. . . pok*ee*toh]
   just there allí mismo [a-y*ee* m*ee*z-moh]
   not just now no en este momento
   just now ahora mismo [ah-*o*ra m*ee*zmoh]
   he was here just now estaba aquí hace un
   momento [. . . ak*ee* ah-theh . . .]
   that's just right así está bién [bee-*e*n]
keep: can I keep it? ¿puedo quedarme con él?
   [pw*e*h-doh keh-d*a*r-meh . . .]
   you keep it quédese con él [keh-deh-seh . . .]
   keep the change quédese con el cambio
   [keh-deh-seh . . .]
   you didn't keep your promise usted no
   cumplió su promesa [o*o*steh noh koomplee-oh
   soo prom-*e*h-sa]
   it keeps on breaking se rompe una y otra
   vez [seh rompeh *oo*na ee *o*-tra veth]
ketchup catsup (de tomate) [kat-s*oo*p . . .]
key la llave [y*a*h-veh]
kidneys los riñones [reen-yoh-ness]
kill mat*a*r
kilo un kilo [k*ee*loh]

» *TRAVEL TIP: conversion:* $\dfrac{kilos}{5} \times 11 = pounds$

kilos	1	1½	5	6	7	8	9
pounds	2.2	3.3	11	13.2	15.4	17.6	19.8

kilometer un kilómetro [keel*o*mmetroh]

» *TRAVEL TIP: conversion:* $\dfrac{kilometers}{8} \times 5 = miles$

kilometers:	1	5	10	20	50	100
miles:	0.62	3.11	6.2	12.4	31	62

kind: that's very kind of you es usted muy
    amable [ess oosteh mwee amah-bleh]
    what kind of...? qué tipo do...?
    [keh teepoh deh...]
kiss un beso [beh-soh]
» TRAVEL TIP: *normal form of greeting between
    female friends and often female and male
    friends*
kitchen cocina [kotheena]
knee una rodilla [rodee-ya]
knife un cuchillo [koochee-yoh]
knock un golpe [−peh]
    **there's a knocking noise from the
    engine** suena un golpeteo en el motor
    [sweh-na oon golpeh-teh-oh...]
know saber [sabair]
    I don't know no sé [noh seh]
    I don't know the area no conozco la región
    [noh konothko la reh-yon]
label una etiqueta [−eekeh-ta]
laces *(shoes)* cordones [kor-doh-ness]
lacquer laca
ladies' restroom los aseos de señoras [ass-eh-oss
    deh sen-yorass]
lady una señora [sehn-yorah]
lager cerveza [thair-veh-tha]
    lager and lime cerveza con lima [...leema]
lamb *(meat)* cordero [−deh]
lamp una lámpara
    lampshade una pantalla [panta-ya]
    lamppost una farola
land *(noun)* tierra [tee-erra]
lane *(car)* el carril [−eel]
language idioma [eed-yoh-ma]
large grande [−deh]
laryngitis laringitis [lareen-heeteess]
last último [ool−]
    last year/week el año pasado/la semana
    pasada [an-yoh...]
    last night anoche [anotcheh]
    at last! ¡al fin! [...feen]

late: sorry I'm late perdone que haya llegado
tarde [pairdoh-neh keh ah-ya yeh-gah-doh
tar-deh]
  it's a bit late es un poco tarde
  please hurry, I'm late dése prisa, por favor,
que llego tarde [deh-seh pree-sa . . . keh yeh-goh
tardeh]
  at the latest a más tardar
  later más tarde
  I'll come back later volveré más tarde
[volveh-reh . . .]
  see you later hasta luego [asta lweh-goh]
latitude latitud [−too]
laugh (verb) reír [reh-eer]
laundrette una lavandería automática [−ree-a
ow-toh-matteeka]
laundry detergent jabón en polvo [habon . . .]
lavabos toilets
law la ley [lay]
lawyer un abogado
laxative un laxante [−teh]
lazy perezoso [peh-rethosoh]
leaf una hoja [oh-ha]
leak un agujero [agoo-heh-roh]
  there's a leak in my ceiling tengo una gotera
en el techo [. . . goh-teh-ra . . .]
  the gas tank leaks se sale la gasolina [seh
sah-leh la gassoh-leena]
learn: I want to learn . . . quiero saber . . .
[kee-eh-roh sab-air]
lease (verb) arrendar
least: not in the least de ninguna manera [deh
neengoona maneh-ra]
  at least por lo menos
leather cuero [kweh-roh]
  this meat's like leather esta carne está como
suela de zapato [. . . karneh . . . sweh-la deh
thapah-toh]
leave: we're leaving tomorrow nos vamos
mañana]

....

when does the bus leave? ¿a qué hora sale
el autobús? [ah keh *ora* s*a*h-leh el ow-toh-b*oo*ss]
I left two shirts in my room me dejé dos
camisas en mi habitación [meh de*h*eh doss
kam*ee*-sass en mee abbee-tath-yon]
can I leave this here? ¿puedo dejar esto
aquí? [pw*e*h-doh de*h*ar *e*stoh ak*ee*]
left izquierdo [eeth-kee-*a*ir-doh]
on the left a la izquierda
left-handed zurdo [th*oor*-doh]
left luggage (office) la consigna de equipajes
[kons*ee*gna deh ekeep*a*h-*h*ess]
leg una pierna [pee-*a*ir-na]
legal legal [leh-g*a*l]
lemon un limón [lee−]
lemonade limonada [lee−]
lend: will you lend me your . . . ? ¿quiere
prestarme su . . . ? [kee-*e*h-reh presst*a*r-meh soo]
lengthen alarg*a*r
lens *(photographic)* el objetivo [ob-*h*eh-t*ee*voh]
Lent Cuaresma [kwar*e*zma]
less menos [m*e*h-noss]
less than three menos de tres [. . . deh . . .]
less than that menos que eso [. . . keh . . .]
let: let me help déjeme ayudarle [d*e*heh-meh
ah-yood*a*r-leh]
let me go! ¡suélteme! [sw*e*ll-teh-meh]
will you let me off here? déjeme aquí, por
favor [d*e*heh-meh ak*ee*]
let's go vámonos [b*a*h-mo-noss]
letter una carta
are there any letters for me? ¿hay cartas
para mí? [eye . . . mee]
lettuce lechuga [−ch*oo*−]
liable *(responsible)* responsable [−s*a*h-bleh]
library una biblioteca [beeb-lee-oh-t*e*h-ka]
license el permiso [pair-m*ee*-soh]
license plate la placa de la matrícula
[−*ee*koo−]
lid la tapa
lie *(noun)* una mentira [−t*ee*−]

can he lie down for a bit? ¿puede acostarse un rato? [pweh-deh akosst*ar*-seh . . .]

life la vida [v*ee*-da]

life insurance un seguro de vida [seh-g*oo*roh . . .]

not at my age! ¡ya estoy viejo para eso! [. . . vee-*eh-ho* . . .]

life jacket un salvavidas [–v*ee*dass]

lifeboat una lancha salvavidas

lifeguard un vigilante [vee*hee*lanteh]

lift: do you want a lift? ¿quiere que le lleve en mi coche? [kee-*eh*-reh keh leh y*eh*-veh en mee k*o*tcheh]

could you give me a lift? ¿podría llevarme en su coche? [pod-r*ee*-ah yeh-v*ar*meh . . .]

light *(noun)* la luz [looth]

the lights aren't working no funcionan las luces [noh foonth-yonan las l*oo*thess]

have you got a light? ¿tiene fuego? [tee-*eh*-neh fw*eh*-goh]

when it gets light cuando se haga de día [kw*a*ndoh seh *ah*-ga deh d*ee*-a]

light bulb una bombilla [–b*ee*ya]

(not heavy) ligero [lee-*heh*-roh]

light meter el fotómetro

like: would you like . . . ? ¿quiere usted . . . ? [kee-*eh*-reh oosteh]

I'd like a . . . /I'd like to . . . quisiera un . . . /quisiera . . . [kees-y*eh*-ra]

I like it/you me gusta/gustas [g*oo*–]

I don't like it no me gusta

what's it like? ¿cómo es?

do it like this hágalo así [*ah*-galoh ass*ee*]

one like this uno como éste

lime lima [l*ee*ma]

line línea [l*ee*-neh-a]

line *(for tickets, etc.)* una cola

» *TRAVEL TIP: don't expect lines of people to be orderly*

lip el labio [l*ah*b-yo]

lipstick una barra de labios

lip salve crema labial
liqueur un licor
» *TRAVEL TIP: Tia Maria: coffee liqueur; 43*
(kwarent-eye-tress): *orange like cointreau; anis:*
aniseed; Marie Brizard: anisette
liquidación sale
list *(noun)* una lista [leesta]
listen escuchar [eskoo−]
liter un litro [leetroh]
» *TRAVEL TIP: 1 liter = 1.06 quarts = 0.26 gallons*
little pequeño [peckehn-yoh]
    a little ice/a little more un poco de hielo/un
    poco más [. . . yeh-loh . . .]
    just a little sólo un poquito [poh-kee-toh]
live vivir [veeveer]; **I live in . . .** vivo en . . .
    where do you live? ¿dónde vive usted?
    [. . . veeveh oosteh]
liver el hígado [eegadoh]
lizard un lagarto
llegadas arrivals
loaf un pan
lobster langosta
local: could we try a local wine? ¿quisiéramos
    probar un vino de la localidad?
    [keess-yeh-ramoss pro-bar oon . . .]
    a local restaurant un restaurante del barrio
    [rest-ow-ranteh del barree-oh]
    is it made locally? ¿se fabrica aquí? [seh
    fabreeka akee]
lock: the lock's broken sa ha roto la cerradura
    [seh ah . . . therradoora]
    I've locked myself out no puedo entrar
    porque me he dejado la llave dentro [noh
    pweh-doh entrar porkeh meh eh deh-hadoh la
    yah-veh dentroh]
London Londres [londress]
lonely solitario [−tar-yoh]
long largo
    we'd like to stay longer nos gustaría
    quedarnos más tiempo [noss goostaree-a
    keh-darnoss mass tee-empoh]

that was long ago eso fue hace mucho
tiempo [. . . fweh *a*h-theh . . .]
longitude longitud [lon-*h*ee-t*oo*]
look: you look tired parece usted cansado
[par*e*h-theh oost*e*h . . .]
  I'm looking forward to . . . tengo muchas
ganas de . . .
  I'm just looking sólo estoy mirando
  I'm looking for . . . estoy buscando . . .
  look at that mire eso [m*ee*-reh *e*h-soh]
  look out! ¡cuidado! [kwee−]
loose suelto [sw*e*ll-toh]
lose perder [paird*ai*r]
  I've lost my . . . he perdido mi . . . [eh
paird*ee*doh mee]
  excuse me, I'm lost oiga, por favor, me he
perdido [*o*y-ga . . .]
lot: a lot/not a lot mucho/no mucho [m*oo*-choh]
  a lot of french fries/wine muchas patatas
/mucho vino
  lots muchos
  a lot more expensive mucho más caro
lotion una loción [loth-yon]
loud fuerte [fw*ai*rteh]
  louder más fuerte
love: I love you te quiero [teh kee-*e*h-roh]
  he's in love est*á* enamorado
  I love this wine me encanta este vino
  do you love me? ¿me quieres? [meh
kee-*e*h-ress]
lovely encantad*o*r
low bajo [b*a*h-*h*oh]
  low beams luces cortas [l*oo*thess . . .]
luck suerte [sw*ai*r-teh]
  good luck! ¡suerte!
lucky: you're lucky tiene suerte [tee-*e*h-neh
sw*ai*r-teh]
  that's lucky! ¡qué suerte!
luggage equipaje [eckee-p*a*h-*h*eh]
lumbago lumbago [loomb*a*h-goh]
lump un bulto [b*oo*l-toh]

lunch el almuerzo [al-mwair-thoh]
» TRAVEL TIP: *lunch normally available 1:30–3:30*
lungs los pulmones [pool-moh-ness]
luxurious lujoso [loo-hoh-soh]
luxury el lujo [loo-hoh]
  a luxury hotel un hotel de lujo
mad loco
madam señora [sen-yora]
made-to-measure hecho a la medida [etcho ah lah medeeda]
magazine una revista [–vee–]
magnificent magnífico
maid una camarera [–reh-ra]
maiden name nombre de soltera [nombreh deh sol-teh-ra] *Spanish women retain their maiden name even when married*
mail correo
  is there any mail for me? ¿hay algún correo para mí? [eye algoon korreh-oh para mee]
  mailbox un buzón [boo-thon]
mainland tierra firme [tee-erra feer-meh]
main road una calle principal [ka-yeh preentheepal]
  (in the country) la carretera principal
make hacer [athair]
  will we make it in time? ¿llegaremos a tiempo? [yeh-gareh-moss ah tee-empoh]
  make-up maquillaje [mackee-yah-heh]
  make-up foundation crema base [kreh-ma bah-seh]
man un hombre [ombreh]
manager el director [dee–]
  can I see the manager? quiero ver al director [kee-eh-roh vair . . .]
manicure manicura [–eekoo–]
manners modales [modah-less]
many muchos [moochoss]
map un mapa
  a map of . . . un mapa de . . . [. . . deh]
March marzo [–thoh]
margarine margarina

marina puerto deportivo [pw*ai*r-toh deport*ee*voh]
mark: there's a mark on it tiene una mancha
  [tee-*e*h-neh . . .]
market un merc*a*do [mair–]
  marketplace el mercado
marmalade mermelada de naranja [mairmeh-
  l*a*h-da deh nar*a*n-h*a*]
married casado
marry: will you marry me? ¿te quieres casar
  conmigo? [teh kee-*e*h-ress kass*a*r konm*ee*goh]
marvelous maravilloso [–veey*o*h-soh]
mascara rímel
mashed potatoes puré de patatas [poor*e*h . . .]
massage masaje [mass*a*h-*h*eh]
mast el m*á*stil
mat una estera
match: a box of matches una caja de cerillas
  [k*a*h-*h*a deh ther*ee*-yass]
material material [matteh-ree-*a*l]
  (cloth) tejido [teh-*h*eedoh]
matter: it doesn't matter no importa
  what's the matter? ¿qué occurre? [keh
  ok*oo*rreh]
mattress un colchón
mature maduro [–d*oo*–]
maximum m*á*ximo
May mayo [m*a*h-yoh]
may: may I have . . . ? ¿me da . . . ? [meh . . .]
maybe tal vez [. . . veth]
mayonnaise mayonesa [mah-yonn*e*h-sa]
me me [meh]
  come with me venga conmigo [. . . –m*ee*goh]
  it's for me es para mí [. . . mee]
  it's me soy yo
meal una comida [komm*ee*da]
mean: what does this mean? ¿qué significa
  esto? [keh signif*ee*kah . . .]
  by all means! ¡naturalmente!
  [natoor*a*lmenteh]
measles sarampión [–y*o*n]
  German measles rubéola [roobeh-ola]

measurements medidas [−d*ee*−]

meat carne [k*a*rneh]

mechanic: is there a mechanic here? ¿hay
algún mecánico aquí? [eye . . . ak*ee*]

medicine una medicina [−th*ee*na]

meet: pleased to meet you mucho gusto (en
conocerle) [m*oo*choh g*oo*stoh (en konoth*ai*r-leh)]
when shall we meet? ¿cuándo nos reunimos?
[kw*a*ndoh noss reh-oon*ee*moss]
I met him in the street me encontré con él
en la calle [meh enkontreh . . . k*a*-yeh]

meeting una reunión [reh-oon-yon]

melon un melón

member socio [s*o*th-yoh]
how do I become a member? ¿cómo puedo
hacerme socio? [. . . pweh-doh ath*ai*rmeh . . .]

men caballeros [kaba-yeh-ross]

mend: can you mend this? ¿puede arregl*a*r
esto? [pweh-deh . . .]

men's restroom los servicios de caballeros
[sair-v*ee*th-yoss deh kabay*e*h-ross]

mention: don't mention it de nada [deh . . .]

menu el menú [men*oo*]
can I have the menu, please? ¿me trae el
menú, por favor? [meh tr*a*h-eh . . .]
see pages 70–71

mess lío [l*ee*-oh]

**message: are there any messages for
me?** ¿hay algún recado para mí? [eye alg*oo*n
reh-k*a*h-doh para mee]
can I leave a message for . . . ? quisiera dejar
un recado para . . . [keess-yeh-ra deh-*ha*r . . .]

meter un metro
» *TRAVEL TIP: 1 meter = 39.37 in. = 1.09 yd.*

metro subway

midday mediodía [mehd-yoh-d*ee*-a]

middle: in the middle en el centro [th−]
in the middle of the road en medio de la
calle [en m*e*hd-yoh . . . k*a*-yeh]

midnight medianoche [meh-dee-ah-n*o*tcheh]

might: I might be late es posible que llegue tarde [ess posse*e*bleh keh y*e*h-gheh t*a*rdeh]
he might have gone es posible que se haya ido [. . . seh *a*h-ya *ee*-doh]
migraine jaqueca [*h*ackeh-ka]
mild suave [sw*a*h-veh]
(weather) templado
mile una milla [m*ee*-ya]

» TRAVEL TIP: conversion: $\frac{miles}{5} \times 8 = kilometers$

miles	½	1	3	5	10	50	100
kilometers	0.8	1.6	4.8	8	16	80	160

milk leche [l*e*h-cheh]
a glass of milk un vaso de leche [b*a*h-soh deh . . .]
milkshake un batido [−t*ee*−]
millimeter un mil*í*metro
millionaire millonario [mee-yon*a*r-yoh]
minced meat carne picada [k*a*rneh . . .]
mind: I've changed my mind he cambiado de idea [eh kamb-y*a*-doh deh eed*e*h-a]
I don't mind me es igual [meh ess eeg-w*a*l]
do you mind if I . . . ? ¿le importa si . . . ? [leh . . .]
never mind ¡qué más da! [keh . . .]
mine mío [m*ee*-oh]
it's mine es mío
mineral water agua mineral [*a*hg-wa meeneh-r*a*l]
minimum m*í*nimo
minus menos [m*e*h-noss]
minus 3 degrees tres grados bajo cero [. . . b*a*h-*h*oh th*e*h-roh]
minute un minuto [−een*oo*−]
in a minute en seguida [segh*ee*-da]
just a minute un momento
mirror un espejo [essp*e*h-*h*oh]
Miss Señorita [sen-yor*ee*ta]
miss: I miss you le echo de menos [leh *e*tchoh deh m*e*h-noss]

Starters
cocktail de gambas *prawn cocktail*
zumo de tomate *tomato juice*
espárragos con mayonesa *asparagus with mayonnaise*
ensalada mixta *mixed salad*
entremeses variados *mixed hors d'oeuvres*
croquetas *croquettes*

Sopas: Soup
gazpacho *refreshingly cold purée of tomato, bread, oil and vinegar + garlic and peppers*
consomé *clear soup*
sopa Juliana *shredded vegetable soup*
sopa sevillana *fish and mayonnaise*
crema de champiñones *cream of mushroom*
sopa de cebolla *onion with bread, cheese*

Verduras: Vegetable dishes
alcachofas salteadas con jamón *sautéed artichokes with ham*
menestra *stew of broad beans and other vegetables*
habas con jamón *broad beans fried with ham*

Carnes: Meat dishes
entrecot a la parrilla *grilled steak*
escalope Milanesa *fried escalope of veal in white sauce and bread-crumbs*
albóndigas *meatballs in sauce*
pierna de cordero *leg of lamb*
chuletas de cerdo *pork chops*
filete de ternera *beef steak*
lomo al ajillo *pork loin in garlic*

Aves y caza: Fowl and game
pollo asado *roast chicken*
gallina en pepitoria *chicken casserole with almonds, garlic, etc.*
pato a la naranja *duck in orange sauce*
perdiz/faisán/codorniz *partridge, pheasant, quail*

Pescado: Fish
merluza *cod*
mero *grouper*
lenguado *sole*
boquerones fritos *fried fresh anchovies*
calamares fritos *squid fried in batter*
calamares en su tinta *squid in its ink*
gambas a la plancha *grilled scampi*
pez espada *swordfish*

Huevos: Egg dishes
tortilla española *potato omelette*
tortilla francesa *plain omelette*
tortilla de jamón *ham omelette*
huevos a la flamenca *eggs baked with tomato,
    ham, onion, asparagus, sausage*
huevos al plato *eggs baked in oven*
huevos fritos con jamón *fried eggs and ham*
arroz a la cubana *fried eggs and banana with
    rice and tomato purée*

Others
paella *rice, shellfish, meat, peas, tomato, red
    peppers and saffron*
fabada asturiana *butter-bean stew*
cocido *chick-pea stew, sausage and vegetables*

Postres: Desserts
fruta del tiempo *seasonal fruit*
piña *pineapple*
melocotón en almíbar *peach in syrup*
flan *caramel custard*
tarta helada *multi-layered ice cream*
pijama *caramel custard, ice cream, fruit and
    syrup*

he is missing falta
    there is a . . . missing falta un/una . . .
mist bruma [br*oo*ma]
mistake una equivocación [eckeevoh-kath-y*on*]
    I think you've made a mistake me parece
    que se ha equivocado usted [meh par*e*h-theh
    keh seh ah eckeevok*a*h-doh oost*e*h]
misunderstanding un malentendido
modern moderno [−d*air*−]
mom mamá
Monday lunes [l*oo*ness]
money dinero [dee-n*e*h-roh]
    I've lost my money se me ha perdido el
    dinero [seh meh ah pair*dee*doh . . .]
    I've no money no tengo dinero
    they've taken all my money se han llevado
    todo mi dinero [seh an yeh-v*a*h-doh t*o*h-doh
    mee deen*e*h-roh]
» *TRAVEL TIP: see* **change**
month un mes [mess]
moon la luna [l*oo*−]
moorings el amarradero
moped un ciclomotor [theekloh−]
more más
    can I have some more? ¿me da un poco más?
    [meh . . .]
    more wine, please más vino, por favor
    no more ya no más
    more comfortable más c*ó*modo
    more than three/that más de tres/que eso
    [. . . deh . . . /keh . . .]
morning la mañana [man-y*a*h-na]
    good morning buenos días [bweh-noss
    d*ee*-ass]
    this morning esta mañana
    in the morning por la mañana
mosquito un mosquito
most: I like it/you the most es el que más me
    gusta/eres quien más me gusta [. . . el keh . . . /
    eh-ress kee-*e*n . . .]

most of the time/the people la mayor parte
del tiempo/la mayoría de la gente [ma-yor
parteh del tee-empo/ma-yoree-a ... henteh]
that's most kind muy amable de su parte
[mwee amah-bleh deh soo parteh]
motel un motel
mother: my mother mi madre [mee mah-dreh]
motor el motor
motorbike una moto
motorboat una motora
motorcyclist un motorista [−ree−]
motorist un automovilista [ow-tomoveeleesta]
mountain una montaña [montahn-ya]
mouse un ratón
moustache bigote [beegoteh]
mouth la boca
move: don't move no se mueva [no seh
mweh-va]
   could you move your car? ¿podría usted
cambiar de sitio su coche? [podree-a oosteh
kamb-yar deh seet-yo soo kotcheh]
movie una película [pelee-koola]
   let's go to the movies vamos al cine
[bamoss al theeneh]
   movie theater el cine [theeneh]
Mr. Señor
Mrs. Señora [sen-yora]
Ms *no exact equivalent in Spanish*
much mucho [mootchoh]
   much better/much more mucho
mejor/mucho más [... meh-hor]
   not much no mucho
muffler el silenciador [seelenth-yador]
mug: I've been mugged me han atacado [meh
an ...]
muscle un músculo [−ooskoo−]
museum un museo [moosseh-oh]
mushrooms champiñones [champeen-yoh-ness]
music música [moosseeka]
must: I must have ... tengo que tomar ...

I must not eat... no debo comer... [noh deh-boh komair]
you must (do it) debe usted de hacerlo [deh-beh oosteh deh athair-loh]
must I...? ¿tengo que...? [...keh]
mustard mostaza [mosstah-tha]
my mi [mee]
nail *finger* una uña [oon-ya]
(wood) un clavo
nailfile una lima para las uñas [leema...]
nail polish esmalte para las uñas [ezmal-teh...]
nail clippers un cortauñas [korta-oon-yass]
nail scissors unas tijeritas de uñas [tee-heh-reetass...]
naked desnudo [dess-noodoh]
name el nombre [−breh]
my name is... me llamo... [meh yah-moh]
what's your name? ¿cómo se llama usted? [...seh yah-ma oosteh]
first name nombre de pila [nombreh deh peela]
napkin una servilleta [sairvee-yeh-ta]
narrow estrecho
national nacional [nath-yonal]
nationality la nacionalidad
natural natural [−too−]
naughty: don't be naughty! ¡no seas malo! [...seh-ass...]
near: it is near? ¿está cerca? [...thair-ka]
near here cerca de aquí [...akee]
do you go near...? ¿va a pasar usted cerca de...? [...oosteh...]
where is the nearest...? ¿dónde está el...más cercano? [...thair-kah-noh]
nearly casi [kah-see]
neat *(drink)* solo
necessary necesario [nethessar-yoh]
it's not necessary no es necesario
neck el cuello [kweh-yoh]
necklace un collar [koy-yar]

need: I need a ... necesito un ...
[nethess*ee*toh]

needle una aguja [ag*oo*-ha]

negotiation negociación [negoth-yath-yon]

neighbor vecino [veth*ee*noh]

neither: neither of them ninguno de los dos
[neeng*oo*noh ...]

neither ... nor ... ni ... ni ... [nee ...]

neither do I ni yo tampoco

nephew: my nephew mi sobrino [mee
sobr*ee*noh]

nervous nervioso [nairv-y*o*soh]

net una red [reth]

net price precio neto [pr*e*th-yoh n*e*h-toh]

never nunca

new nuevo [nw*e*h-voh]

New Year Año Nuevo [*a*n-yoh]

New Year's Eve Nochevieja [n*o*tcheh
vee-*e*h-ha]

Happy New Year Feliz Año Nuevo
[feh-l*ee*th ...]

*In Spain it is traditional to swallow one grape
on each stroke of midnight*

news noticias [noh-t*ee*th-yass]

newsstand una tienda de periódicos [tee-*e*nda
deh peh-ree-*o*ddeekoss]

newspaper un periódico

do you have any English newspapers?
¿tiene usted algún periódico inglés? [tee-*e*h-neh
oost*e*h alg*oo*n peh-ree-*o*ddeekoh eengl*e*ss]

New Zealand Nueva Zelanda [nw*e*h-va
theh-l*a*nda]

New Zealander neozelandés [neh-o-theh-land*e*ss]

next próximo

sit next to me siéntese a mi lado
[see-*e*nteh-seh ...]

please stop at the next corner haga el favor
de parar en la esquina próxima [*a*h-ga ...
esk*ee*na ...]

see you next year hasta el año que viene
[*a*sta el *a*n-yoh keh vee-*e*h-neh]

next week/next Tuesday la semana/el martes que viene

nice agradable [−dah-bleh]

niece: my niece mi sobrina [mee sobreena]

night noche [notcheh]

   goodnight buenas noches [bweh-nass notchess]

   at night por la noche

   is there a good nightclub here? ¿dónde hay un buen "nightclub"? [dondeh eye oon bwen . . .]

   night life vida nocturna [veeda noctoorna]

   night porter el portero [porteh-roh]

no no

   there's no water no hay agua [noh eye ahg-wa]

   no way! ¡de ninguna manera! [. . . maneh-ra]

   I have no money no tengo dinero [deeneh-roh]

no potable *not for drinking*

nobody nadie [nahd-yeh]

   nobody saw it nadie lo vió [. . . vee-oh]

noisy ruidoso [rweedosoh]

   our room is too noisy se oye demasiado ruido en nuestra habitación [seh o-yeh demass-yah-doh rweedoh en nwestra abbee-tath-yon]

none ninguno

   none of them ninguno de ellos [neengoonoh deh eh-yoss]

nonsense tonterías [−ree-ass]

normal normal

north norte [−teh]

Northern Ireland Irlanda del Norte [. . . norteh]

nose la nariz [−eeth]; **nosebleed** una hemorragia nasal [emmorah-hee-ah nassal]

not no

   I'm not hungry no tengo hambre [. . . ambreh]

   not that one eso no [eh-seh . . .]

   not me yo no

I don't understand no entiendo [. . . ent-
yendoh]
  he didn't tell me no me lo dijo [. . . meh loh
  dee-hoh]
nothing nada
November noviembre [novee-embreh]
now ahora [ah-ora]
nowhere en ningún sitio [en neengoon seet-yoh]
nudist nudista [noodeesta]
  nudist beach una playa nudista [plah-ya . . .]
nuisance: it's a nuisance es una lata
  this man is being a nuisance este hombre
  me está molestando [. . . ombreh meh . . .]
numb entumecido [entoomeh-theedoh]
number un número [noo–]
  see pages 124–125
nurse una enfermera [emfair-meh-ra]
nut una nuez [nweth]
  (for bolt) una tuerca [twairka]
oar un remo [reh-moh]
objetos perdidos *lost property*
obligatory obligatorio [obleegator-yoh]
obras *roadway construction*
obviously evidentemente [–teh]
occasionally de vez en cuando [deh veth en
  kwandoh]
occupied ocupado
o'clock *see* **time**
October octubre [oktoobreh]
octopus un pulpo [pool–]
ocupado *occupied*
odd *(number)* impar [eem–]
  (strange) raro [rah–]
odometer el cuentakilómetros [kwenta . . .]
of de [deh]
off: it just came off se ha soltado sin más [seh
  ah . . .]
  10% off un descuento del diez por ciento [oon
  dess-kwentoh del dee-eth por thee-entoh]
offense un insulto [eensooltoh]
  (legal) una infracción [eemfrakth-yon]

....

office la oficina [−eeth*ee*−]

officer *(to policeman)* agente [a*h*enteh]

official *(noun)* un funcionario
[foonth-yon*a*h-ree-oh]

often a menudo [ah men*oo*doh]

oil aceite [ath*a*y-teh]
   I'm losing oil estoy perdiendo aceite
   [. . . pairdee-endoh . . .]
   will you change the oil? ¿quiere cambiar el
   aceite? [kee-*eh*-reh kamb-y*a*r . . .]

ointment pomada

OK! ¡vale! [b*a*h-leh]

old viejo [vee-*eh*-*h*oh]
   how old are you? ¿cuántos años tienes?
   [kw*a*ntoss *a*n-yoss tee-*eh*-ness]

olive una aceituna [ath*a*y-t*oo*na]
   olive oil aceite de oliva [ath*a*y-teh deh ol*ee*va]

omelette una tortilla [tort*ee*ya]

on en
   I haven't got it on me no lo llevo encima
   [. . . y*eh*-vo enth*ee*-ma]
   on Friday el viernes [. . . vee-*a*irness]
   on television en la tele [. . . t*eh*-leh]

once una vez [veth]
   at once en seguida [seh-gh*ee*da]

one uno [*oo*no]
   the red one el rojo [r*o*-ho]

one-way: a one-way ticket to . . . un billete
   para . . . [. . . beel-y*eh*-teh . . .]

onion una cebolla [theh-b*o*y-ya]

only *(adjective)* único [*oo*neekoh]
   only one sólo uno
   only once sólo una vez [. . . veth]

open *(adjective)* abierto [ab-y*a*irtoh]
   I can't open it no puedo abrirlo [noh
   pw*eh*-doh abr*ee*rloh]
   when do you open? ¿a qué hora abre?
   [ah keh *o*ra *a*h-breh]

opera la ópera

operation una operación [−ath-y*o*n]

will I need an operation? ¿necesitaré una
operación? [nethesseetareh . . .]
operator *(tel)* la operadora
» TRAVEL TIP: *dial 009 (national) or 008
(international)*
opposite: opposite the hotel enfrente del hotel
[emfrenteh del o-tel]
optician una óptica
or o
orange naranja [naran-ha]
orange juice zumo de naranja [thoo-moh . . .]
order: could we order now? ¿podemos pedir ya
la comida? [podeh-moss pedeer yah la komeeda]
thank you, we've already ordered gracias,
ya hemos pedido [. . . yah eh-moss pedeedoh]
other: the other one el otro
do you have any others? ¿tiene usted más de
estos? [tee-eh-neh oosteh . . .]
(different ones) ¿tiene usted otros distintos?
otherwise de otra manera
ought: I ought to go debería irme [deberee-a
eer-meh]
ounce una onza [ontha]
» TRAVEL TIP: *1 ounce = 28.35 grams*
our nuestro [nwesstroh]
that's ours eso es nuestro
out: we're out of gas se nos ha acabado la
gasolina [seh noss ah . . .]
get out! ¡fuera! [fweh-ra]
outboard *(motor)* fuera-bordo
outdoors fuera de casa
outlet *(electrical)* una toma de corriente
[. . . korr-yenteh]
outside: can we sit outside? ¿podemos
sentarnos fuera? [podeh-moss . . .]
over: over here/there aquí/allá [akee/a-ya]
over 40 más de cuarenta [. . . kwarenta]
it's all over ¡se acabó!
overboard: man overboard! ¡hombre al agua!
[ombreh al ahg-wa]

overcharge: you've overcharged me me ha
cobrado de más [meh ah . . .]
overcooked recocido [reh-koth*ee*doh]
overexposed sobreexpuesto
[soh-breh-esspw*e*ssto]
overnight *(travel)* durante la noche [doo– . . .]
oversleep dormir demasiado [dorm*ee*r
demass-y*a*h-doh]
   I overslept se me han pegado las sábanas
   [seh meh an . . .]
overtake adelant*a*r
owe: what do I owe you? ¿cuánto le debo?
[kw*a*ntoh leh d*e*h-boh]
own *(adjective)* propio [proh-pee-oh]
   my own . . . mi propio . . .
   I'm on my own estoy solo [estoy-pee-eh-t*a*r-yoh]
owner el propietario [proh-pee-eh-t*a*r-yoh]
oxygen oxígeno [ox*ee*-*h*eh-noh]
oyster una ostra
pack: I haven't packed yet todavía no he hecho
las maletas [tohda-v*ee*-a noh eh *e*tchoh . . .]
page *(of book)* página [p*a*h-*h*eena]
   could you page him? ¿podría llamarle por
   los altavoces? [podr*ee*-a yam*a*rleh por loss
   altavothess]
pain dolor
   I've got a pain in my . . . me duele el . . .
   [meh dw*e*h-leh . . .]
   painkillers calmantes [kalm*a*ntess]
painting un cuadro [kw*a*droh]
pajamas el pijama [pee-*h*a-ma]
pale pálido
pancake una crêpe [krep]
panties las bragas
pants los pantalones [–*o*-ness]
paper papel
   (newspaper) un periódico [peh-ree-*o*ddeekoh]
parada stop (bus etc.)
paraffin parafina [–f*ee*–]
parcel un paquete [pak*e*h-teh]
pardon? *(didn't understand)* ¿cómo?

I beg your pardon (sorry) usted perdone [oosteh pairdoh-neh]

parents: my parents mis padres [meess pah-dress]

park el parque [parkeh]

where can I park my car? ¿dónde puedo aparcar el coche? [dondeh pweh-doh ... kotcheh]

parking lot un aparcamiento [–mee-entoh]

part una parte [–teh]

partner pareja [pareh-ha]

party (group) un grupo [groo–] (celebration) una fiesta

I'm with the ... party estoy en el grupo de ...

pasen cross

paso a nivel grade crossing

pass (mountain) un puerto [pwairtoh]

he's passed out ha perdido el conocimiento [ah pairdeedoh el konotheem-yentoh]

passable (road) transitable [–eetah-bleh]

passenger un pasajero [passa-heh-roh]

passerby un transeúnte [tran-seh-oonteh]

passport pasaporte [passaporteh]

past: in the past antiguamente [anteegwa-menteh]

pastry masa (cakes) pastelillos [pastel-eeyoss]

path un camino [–mee–]

patient: be patient tenga paciencia [... path-yenth-ya]

pattern (on cloth, etc.) dibujo [dee-boo-hoh]

pavement la acera [atheh-ra]

pay pagar

can I pay, please? ¿me puede cobrar, por favor? [meh pweh-deh ...]

peace paz [path]

peach un melocotón

peaje toll

peanut un cacahuete [kacka-weh-teh]

pear una pera [peh-ra]

peas guisantes [ghee-sahn-tess]
peatones *pedestrians*
pebble. un guijarro [ghee-harroh]
pedal *(noun)* un pedal
pedestrian un peatón [peh-ah-tonn]
   pedestrian crossing un paso de peatones
   [–ness]
» *TRAVEL TIP: beware! cars don't always stop*
peg una pinza [peen-tha]
   (tent) una estaca
peligro *danger*
peligro de incendio *danger of fire*
pelvis la pelvis [–eess]
pen una pluma [plooma]
   have you got a pen? ¿tiene un bolígrafo?
   [tee-eh-neh oon boleegrafoh]
pencil un lápiz [lapeeth]
penicillin penicilina [peneetheeleena]
penknife una navaja [navah-ha]
pen pal amigo por correspondencia
   [...denth-ya]
pensioner un pensionista [penss-yoneesta]
people gente [henteh]
   the Spanish people los españoles
   [esspan-yoless]
pepper *(spice)* pimienta [peem-yenta]
   (vegetable) pimiento
peppermint menta
per: per night/week/person por
   noche/semana/persona
percent por ciento [...thee-entoh]
perfect perfecto [pair–]
   the perfect vacation las vacaciones perfectas
   [vakath-yoness]
perfume perfume [pairfoomeh]
perhaps quizás [keethass]
period *(also menstruation)* el período
   [peh-ree-odoh]
permanent *(hair)* una permanente
   [pairmanenteh]
permit *(noun)* un permiso [pair-meesoh]

PLATE 83

person una persona [pair–]
  in person en persona
pharmacy una farmacia [far-m*a*th-ya]
phone *see* **telephone**
photograph una foto
  would you take a photograph of us? ¿le
  importaría hacernos una foto? [leh
  eemportar*ee*-ah ath*ai*r-noss . . .]
piano un piano
pickpocket un ratero
piece un pedazo [ped*a*h-thoh]
  a piece of . . . un pedazo de . . .
pig un cerdo [th*ai*r-doh]
pigeon una paloma
pile-up un accidente múltiple [ak-theed*e*nteh
  m*oo*lteepleh]
pill una píldora
  do you take the pill? ¿toma la píldora?
pillow una almohada [almoh-*a*h-da]
pin un alfiler [alfee-l*ai*r]
pineapple piña [p*ee*n-ya]
pint una pinta [p*ee*nta]
» *TRAVEL TIP: 1 pint = 0.47 liters*
pipe una pipa [p*ee*pa]
  pipe tobacco tabaco de pipa
piso floor
piston un pistón
pity: it's a pity es una lástima
place un sitio [s*ee*t-yoh]
  is this place taken? ¿está ocupado este sitio?
  do you know any good places to go? ¿sabe
  de sitios buenos adonde ir? [s*a*h-beh . . .
  bw*e*h-noss adondeh eer]
plain *(food)* sencilla [sen-th*ee*ya]
  (not patterned) liso [l*ee*-soh]
plane un avión [av-yon]
plant una planta
plastic plástico
  plastic bag una bolsa de plástico
  plastic wrap celofán [the-loh-f*a*n]
plate un plato .

platform el andén
  which platform, please? ¿qué andén, por
  favor? [keh...]
play: *(verb)* jugar [*hoogar*]
pleasant agradable [−d*ah*-bleh]
please: could you please...? ¿podría hacer el
  favor de...? [podr*ee*-ah ath*air*...]
  (yes) please por favor
pleasure placer [plath-*air*]
  it's my pleasure no hay de qué [no eye deh
  keh]
plenty: plenty of... mucho... [moo−]
  thank you, that's plenty ya basta, gracias
pliers unos alicates [−*ah*-tess]
plug *(electric)* un enchufe [ench*oo*feh]
  (bathroom) el tapón
plum una ciruela [theer-w*eh*-la]
plumber el fontanero
plus más
p.m. de la tarde *see* **a.m.**
pneumonia neumonía [neh-oo-mon*ee*-a]
poached egg un huevo escalfado [w*eh*-voh...]
pocket un bolsillo [bols*ee*-yoh]
point: could you point to it? ¿puede señalarlo?
  [pw*eh*-deh senyal*a*rloh]
  four point six cuatro coma seis [kw*a*troh
  k*o*ma sayss]
  points *(car)* los platinos [−t*ee*−]
police la policía [−th*ee*-a]
  get the police llame a la policía [y*ah*-meh...]
  policeman un policía
  police station la comisaría [−r*ee*-a]
» *TRAVEL TIP: dial 091; the national police wear a
  brown uniform with a beret*
polish *(noun)* betún [−t*oo*n]
  will you polish my shoes? ¿quiere limpiarme
  los zapatos? [kee-*eh*-reh leemp-y*a*rmeh loss
  thap*ah*-toss]
» *TRAVEL TIP: you can have your shoes cleaned in
  the street by traveling "limpiabotas"*
polite fino [f*ee*noh]

politics la política [−lee−]
polluted contaminado
pool *(swimming)* una piscina [peess-theena]
poor: I'm very poor soy muy pobre [... mwee
poh-breh]
   poor quality de baja calidad [bah-ha ...]
popular popular [−poo−]
population la población [−ath-yon]
pork carne de cerdo [kar-neh deh thair-doh]
port un puerto [pwairtoh]
   (drink) un Oporto
   to port a babor
porter *(for luggage)* un mozo [moh-thoh]
portrait un retrato
posh *(restaurant)* de lujo [loo-hoh]
possible posible [posseebleh]
   could you possibly ...? ¿le sería posible ...?
[leh serree-ah ...]
postcard una postal
post office la oficina de Correos
[offee-theena ...]
   general delivery la lista de Correos [leesta
deh korreh-oss]
» *TRAVEL TIP: look for the sign "correos"; mailboxes are yellow; letters for abroad in slit marked "extranjero"; see stamps*
potato una patata
   potato chips patatas fritas a la inglesa
[freetass]
pottery cerámica [th−]
pound *(weight)* una libra [leebra]
» *TRAVEL TIP: conversion:* $\dfrac{pounds}{11} \times 5 = kilos$

pounds	1	3	5	6	7	8	9
kilos	0.45	1.4	2.3	2.7	3.2	3.6	4.1

pour: it's pouring está lloviendo a cántaros
[yov-yendoh ...]
powder polvo
   (face) polvos para la cara
power outage un apagón
prawns gambas

precaución *caution*
prefer: I prefer this one prefiero éste
  [pref-yeh-roh essteh]
pregnant embarazada [−athah-da]
prescription una receta [reh-theh-ta]
present: at present actualmente
  [aktwal-menteh]
  present company excepted mejorando lo
  presente [meh-horandoh lo press-enteh]
  here's a present for you le traigo un regalo
  [leh try-goh oon regah-loh]
president el presidente [−teh]
press: could you press these? ¿puede
  planchármelos? [pweh-deh . . . −meh-loss]
pretty mono
  it's pretty good es bastante bueno
  [. . . bwen-noh]
price el precio [preth-yoh]
priest un sacerdote [sathair-doteh]
principio de autopista *start of freeway*
printed matter impresos
prioridad a la derecha *priority to the right*
prison la cárcel [−thel]
private privado
probably probablemente [probah-bleh-menteh]
problem un problema
product un producto [−doo−]
profit una ganancia [gananth-ya]
prohibido *forbidden*
  prohibido adelantar *no passing*
  prohibido aparcar *no parking*
  prohibido el paso *no trespassing*
  prohibido fumar *no smoking*
promise: do you promise? ¿lo promete?
  [pro-meh-teh]
  I promise lo prometo
**pronounce: how do you pronounce
  this?** ¿cómo se pronuncia esto?
  [. . . pronoonth-ya . . .]
propeller una hélice [ellee-theh]
properly correctamente [−teh]

property propiedad [proh-pee-eh-d*a*]
prostitute una prostituta [−t*oo*ta]
protect proteger [pro-teh-*hair*]
Protestant protestante [−teh]
proud orgulloso [orgoo-yosoh]
prove: I can prove it puedo probarlo
  [pweh-doh . . .]
public: the public el público [p*oo*−]
» *TRAVEL TIP: public holidays*
  Jan. 1 Año Nuevo *New Year's Day*
  Jan. 6 Día de Reyes *Epiphany*
  Mar. 19 San José *Saint Joseph*
        Viernes Santo *Good Friday*
        Lunes de Pascua *Easter Monday*
  May 1 Día del Trabajo *Labor Day*
        Corpus Christi *Corpus Christi*
  Jun. 24 Onomástica del Rey *King's St. Day*
  Jul. 25 Día de Santiago *Saint James*
  Aug. 15 Día de la Asunción *Assumption*
  Oct. 12 Día de la Hispanidad *Columbus Day*
  Nov. 1 Todos los Santos *All Saints Day*
  Dec. 8 Inmaculada Concepción *Immaculate
        Conception*
  Dec. 25 Navidad *Christmas*
pudding pudín [pood*een*]
pull *(verb)* tirar de [tee−]
  he pulled out in front of me salió delante de
  mí sin mirar [sal-*y*oh deh-l*a*nteh deh mee seen
  meer*a*r]
pump la bomba
punctual puntual [poont-w*a*l]
puncture un pinchazo [peen-ch*a*-thoh]
pure puro [p*oo*roh]
purple púrpura [p*oo*r-poora]
purse el monedero
push *(verb)* empujar [empoo-*h*ar]
put: where can I put . . . ? ¿dónde puedo
  poner . . . ? [dondeh pweh-doh pon-*air*]
  where have you put . . . ? ¿dónde ha
  puesto . . . ? [. . . ah pw*e*sstoh]
quality calidad [−d*a*]

quarantine cuarentena [kwarenteh-na]
   quarter la cuarta parte [kwarta parteh]
   a quarter of an hour un cuarto de hora
   [kwartoh deh ora]
quay el muelle [mweh-yeh]
question una pregunta [−goo−]
quick rápido; **that was quick** sí que ha sido
   rápido [see keh ah seedoh . . .]
quiet tranquilo [−keeloh]
   be quiet! ¡cállese! [ka-yeh-seh]
quite *(fairly)* bastante [−teh]
   (very) completamente [−teh]
   quite a lot bastante
race *(sport: noun)* una carrera
radiator el radiador [raddeeah−]
radio la radio [rahd-yoh]
rail: by rail en tren
rain la lluvia [yoov-ya]
   it's raining está lloviendo [. . . yov-yendoh]
   raincoat un impermeable
   [eem-pair-meh-ah-bleh]
rally *(car)* rallye
rape una violación [vee-olath-yon]
rare poco común [. . . komoon]
   (steak) poco hecho [. . . etchoh]
raspberry frambuesa [fram-bweh-sa]
rat una rata
rather: I'd rather sit here prefiero sentarme
   aquí [pref-yeh-roh sentarmeh akee]
   I'd rather not prefiero no hacerlo
   [. . . athair-loh]
   it's rather hot hace bastante calor
   [ah-theh . . .]
raw crudo [kroodoh]
razor una maquinilla de afeitar [mackee-nee-ya
   deh affay-tar]
   razor blades hojas de afeitar [o-hass . . .]
read: you read it léalo usted [leh-ah-loh oosteh]
   something to read algo para leer [. . . leh-air]
ready: when will it be ready? ¿cuándo estará
   listo? [kwandoh estara leestoh]

I'm not ready yet aún no estoy listo [ah-*oo*n noh esst*o*y l*ee*stoh]

real verdadero [vair-da-d*e*h-roh]

really realmente [reh-al-m*e*nteh]

rearview mirror el (espejo) retrovisor [essp*e*h-*h*oh retroh-v*ee*sor]

reasonable razonable [rathon*a*h-bleh]

rebajas sale

receipt un recibo [reth*ee*-boh]

can I have a receipt, please? por favor, ¿me da un recibo?

recently recientemente [reth-y*e*nteh-m*e*nteh]

reception *(hotel)* Recepción [rethepth-yon]

at a reception un Recepción

receptionist recepcionista [−*ee*sta]

recién pintado wet paint

recipe una receta [reth*e*h-ta]

recommend: can you recommend...? ¿puede usted recomendar...? [pw*e*h-oost*e*h...]

record *(music)* un disco [d*ee*−]

red rojo [roh-*h*oh]

reduction un descuento [dess-kw*e*ntoh]

refrigerator el frigorífico

refuse: I refuse me niego [meh-nee-*e*h-goh]

region una zona [th*o*-na]

registered letter una carta certificada [...thair-teefeek*a*h-da]

regret: I have no regrets no me arrepiento [noh meh arrep-y*e*ntoh]

relax: I just want to relax sólo quiero descansar [...kee-*e*h-roh...]

relax! ¡tranquilo! [tran-k*ee*loh]

remember: don't you remember? ¿no se acuerda usted? [noh seh akw*ai*rda oost*e*h]

I'll always remember siempre (lo) recordaré [see-*e*mpreh reh-kord*a*-r*e*h]

something to remember you by algún recuerdo suyo [alg*oo*n reh-kw*ai*rdoh s*oo*yoh]

RENFE = Red Nacional de Ferrocarriles Españoles National Railway

rent: can I rent a car/boat/bicycle? ¿puedo alquilar un coche/un barco/una bicicleta? [pweh-doh alkeel*ar* oon k*o*tcheh/ ... beetheekl*e*h-ta]

repair: can you repair it? ¿puede arreglarlo? [pw*e*h-deh ...]

repeat: could you repeat that? ¿puede repetir eso? [pw*e*h-deh reh-pet*ee*r ...]

reputation fama [f*a*h-ma]

rescue *(verb)* rescatar

reservation una reserva [−s*air*−]

   I want to make a reservation for ... quiero hacer una reserva para ... [kee-*e*h-roh ath-*air* ...]

reserve: can I reserve a seat? ¿puedo reservar un asiento? [pw*e*h-doh reh-sair-v*a*r oon assy*e*ntoh]

   I'd like to reserve a table for two quisiera reservar una mesa para dos personas [keess-y*e*h-ra ...]

responsible responsable [−s*a*h-bleh]

rest: I've come here for a rest he venido aquí para descans*ar* [eh ven*ee*doh ak*ee* ...]

   you keep the rest quédese con la diferencia [k*e*h-deh-seh kon la deefer*e*nth-ya]

restaurant un restaurante [rest-ow-r*a*nteh]

rest room los aseos [ass-*e*h-oss]

   where is the rest room? ¿dónde están los aseos?

   public rest room aseos públicos

» *TRAVEL TIP: see* **toilet**

retail price el precio de venta [pr*e*th-yoh ...]

retired jubilado [*h*oobeel*a*h-doh]

retrete toilet

reverse gear la marcha atrás

rheumatism reúma [reh-*oo*ma]

rib una costilla [kost*ee*ya]

rice arroz [arr*o*th]

rich rico [r*ee*koh]

   (cake) empalagoso

ridiculous ridículo [reed*ee*kooloh]

right: that's right eso es
  you're right tiene usted razón [tee-*eh*-neh oost*eh* rathon]
  on the right a la derecha
  right now ahora mismo [ah-*orah* m*ee*z-moh]
  right here aquí mismo [ak*ee*...]
  right-hand drive con el volante a la derecha [... vol*a*nteh...]
ring *(on finger)* una sortija [sor-*tee-h*a]
ripe maduro [−d*oo*−]
rip-off: it's a rip-off es un timo [...t*ee*moh]
river un río [*ree*-oh]
road la carretera
  which is the road to...? ¿cuál es la carretera de...? [kwal ess la karret*eh*-ra deh]
  roadhog un loco del volante [...−teh]
rob: I've been robbed! ¡me han robado! [meh an...]
rock *(noun)* una roca
  whisky on the rocks whisky con hielo [...y*eh*-loh]
roll *(bread)* un panecillo [paneh-th*ee*yoh]
Roman Catholic católico
romantic romántico
roof el tejado [te*h*ah-doh]
room la habitación [abee-tath-yon]
  have you got a single/double room? ¿tiene una habitación individual/doble? [tee-*eh*-neh...eendeeveed-wal/dobleh]
  for one night/for three nights para una noche/para tres noches [...n*o*tcheh...]
  YOU MAY THEN HEAR...
  lo siento, está lleno [loh see-*e*ntoh, est*a* yeh-noh] *sorry, we're full up*
room service servicio de habitaciones [sair-v*ee*th-yoh deh abbee-tath-y*o*ness]
rope una cuerda [kw*air*-da]
rose una rosa [roh-sa]
rough *(sea, weather)* revuelto [reh-vw*e*l-toh]
roughly *(approximately)* aproximadamente [−teh]

....

roulette la ruleta [rool*eh*-ta]
round *(circular)* redondo
**round-trip: a round-trip ticket/two round-trip
tickets to...** un billete/dos billetes de ida y
vuelta a... [...beey*eh*-teh...deh *ee*da ee
vw*e*lta]
roundabout *(traffic)* un cruce en glorieta
[kr*oo*-theh en glor-y*eh*-ta]
route una ruta [r*oo*ta]
   which is the prettiest/fastest route? ¿cuál es
   la ruta más bonita/más rápida? [kwal...]
rowboat un barco de remos [...r*eh*-moss]
rubber goma
   rubber band una goma elástica
rudder el timón
rude grosero [groh-s*eh*-roh]
ruin *(noun)* una ruina [rw*ee*na]
rum ron
   rum and Coke un Cubalibre de ron
   [koobal*ee*breh deh...]
run: hurry, run! ¡corra, dese prisa! [...d*eh*-seh
pr*ee*-sa]
   I've run out of gas/money se me ha acabado
   la gasolina/el dinero [seh meh ah
   ackab*a*h-doh...]
sad triste [tr*ee*ss-teh]
safe seguro [–g*oo*–]
   will it be safe here? ¿estará seguro aquí
   [...ak*ee*]
   is it safe to swim here? ¿se puede nadar sin
   peligro aquí? [seh pw*e*h-deh nad*a*r seen
   pel*ee*groh ak*ee*]
safety seguridad [segoor*ee*da]
   safety pin un imperdible [eem-pair-d*ee*bleh]
sail una vela [v*eh*-la]
   can we go sailing? ¿podemos hacer vela?
   [pod*eh*-moss ath-*air*...]
sailor un marinero [maree-n*eh*-roh]
   (sport) un marino
sala de espera waiting room
salad la ensalada

saldos *sale*
sale: is it for sale? ¿se vende? [seh vendeh]
salida *exit*
salidas *departures*
salmon salmón [sal-mon]
salt sal
same mismo [meez-moh]
   the same again, please lo mismo otra vez,
   por favor [. . . veth . . .]
   the same to you igualmente [eeg-wal-menteh]
   it's all the same to me me es igual [meh ess
   eeg-wal]
sand arena [areh-na]
sandal una sandalia [–al-ya]
sandwich sandwich
» *TRAVEL TIP: a "sandwich" will be toasted;*
   otherwise ask for "un bocadillo" [–deeyoh]
sanitary napkin una compresa
satisfactory satisfactorio [–tor-yoh]
Saturday sábado
sauce salsa
   saucepan un cazo [kah-thoh]
saucer un platillo [–eeyoh]
sauna una sauna [sah-oo-na]
sausage una salchicha [–chee–]
save *(life)* salvar
say: how do you say . . . in Spanish? ¿cómo se
   dice . . . en español? [. . . seh dee-theh . . .]
   what did he say? ¿qué ha dicho? [keh ah
   dee-choh]
scarf una bufanda [boo–]
   (head) un pañuelo [pan-yweh-loh]
scenery el paisaje [pye-saheh]
schedule un programa
   on/behind schedule en punto/con retraso
   scheduled flight vuelo regular [vweh-loh
   regoolar]
school la escuela [ess-kweh-la]
scissors: a pair of scissors unas tijeras [tee-
   heh-rass]
scooter una moto

....

Scotland Escocia [eskoth-ya]
Scottish escocés [eskothess]
scrambled eggs huevos revueltos [weh-voss
   rev-weltoss]
scratch *(verb)* arañar [aran-yar]
scream un chillido [chee-yeedoh]
screw *(noun)* un tornillo [torneeyoh]
   screwdriver un destornillador
   [dess-torneeyador]
se alquila habitación room for rent
   se prohibe la entrada no admission/no entry
   se vende for sale
sea el mar
   by the sea junto al mar [hoontoh . . .]
seafood mariscos [−ree−]
search *(verb)* buscar [boo−]
   search party una expedición de búsqueda
   [oona esspedeeth-yon deh booss-keh-da]
seasick: I feel seasick estoy mareado
   [. . . marreh-ah-doh]
   I get seasick me mareo [meh marreh-oh]
seaside la orilla del mar [oreeya . . .]
   let's go to the seaside vámonos a la playa
   [. . . pla-ya]
season la temporada
   in the high/low season en la temporada
   alta/baja [. . . bahah]
seasoning condimento
seat el asiento [assee-entoh]
   is this somebody's seat? ¿es de alguien este
   asiento? [ess deh alg-yen . . .]
   seat belt cinturón de seguridad [theentooron
   deh segooreeda]
sea urchin un erizo de mar [erree-thoh deh mar]
seaweed algas
second *(adjective)* segundo [−goo−]
   (time) un segundo
   just a second! ¡un momento!
   secondhand de segunda mano
   the second of . . . el dos de . . .
see ver [vair]

....

oh, I see ah, ya comprendo
have you seen...? ¿ha visto usted...?
[ah-ve*e*stoh oost*e*h]
can I see the room? ¿puedo ver la
habitación? [pweh-doh vair la abbee-tath-yon]
seem parecer [pareh-th*air*]
  it seems so eso parece [*e*h-soh par*e*h-theh]
  seldom rara vez [. . . veth]
self: self-service autoservicio
[*o*w-toh-sair-v*e*eth-yoh]
sell vender [vend-*air*]
send enviar [embee-*ar*]
sensitive sensible [sens*ee*bleh]
sentimental sentimental
señoras *ladies*
separate *(adjective)* separado
  I'm separated estoy separado
  can we pay separately? ¿podemos pag*ar* por
separado? [pod*e*h-moss . . .]
September septiembre [septee-*e*mbreh]
serious serio [s*e*h-ree-oh]
  I'm serious lo digo en serio [. . . d*ee*goh . . .]
  this is serious esto es grave [. . . gr*a*h-veh]
  is it serious, doctor? ¿es grave, Doctor?
service: the service was excellent/poor el
servicio ha sido excelente/ha dejado bastante
que desear [el sair-v*e*eth-yoh ah s*e*edoh
esstheh-l*e*nteh/ah deh-*h*ah-doh bass-t*a*nteh keh
desseh-*ar*]
  service station una estación de servicio
[esstath-yon deh sair-v*e*eth-yoh]
servicios *toilets*
several varios [v*a*r-yoss]
sexy sexy
shade: in the shade a la sombra
shake sacudir [sakood*e*er]
  to shake hands estrecharse la mano
[. . . –seh . . .]
» *TRAVEL TIP: shake hands every time you are
introduced to someone, or when you see
someone after an absence*

shallow poco profundo [. . . –foon-doh]
shame: what a shame! ¡qué lástima! [keh . . .]
shampoo *(noun)* el champú [champoo]
share *(room, table)* compartir [–teer]
shark un tiburón [teebooron]
sharp afilado
  (taste) ácido [athee-doh]
shave afeitarse [affay-tarseh]
  shaver máquina de afeitar [mackeena deh affay-tar]
  shaving cream espuma de afeitar
she ella [eh-ya]
  does she live here? vive aquí? [vee-veh akee]
  she is my friend es mi amiga [. . . mee . . .]
  she is tired está cansada
sheep una oveja [oveh-ha]
sheet una sábana
  you haven't changed my sheets no me ha cambiado las sábanas [noh meh ah kambee-ah-doh . . .]
shelf un estante [–teh]
shell una concha
  shellfish mariscos [–ree–]
shelter *(noun)* cobijo [kobee-hoh]
sherry un jerez [hereth]
shin la espinilla [esspeeneeya]
ship un barco
  by ship en barco
shirt una camisa [kamee-sa]
shock *(noun: surprise)* un susto [soo–]
  what a shock! ¿qué susto! [keh . . .]
  I got an electric shock from the . . . me ha dado un calambre el . . . [meh ah dah-doh . . . kalambreh . . .]
  shock absorber un amortiguador [amorteegwador]
shoes zapatos [tha–]
» *TRAVEL TIP: shoe sizes*

	women's					
US	5	6	7	8	9	10
Spain	36	37	38	39	40	41

	men's					
US	7	8	9	10	11	12
Spain	39½	41	42	43	44½	46

shop una tienda [tee–]
  I have some shopping to do tengo que hacer unas compras [. . . keh ath-*air* . . .]
shore la orilla [or*ee*ya]
short corto
  I'm three short me faltan tres [meh . . .]
  short cut un atajo [at*ah*-*h*oh]
shorts pantalones cortos [–oness . . .]
shoulder el hombro [ombroh]
shout grit*a*r [gree–]
show: please show me por favor, enséñeme [. . . ensen-yeh-meh]
shower: with shower con ducha [d*oo*tcha]
shrimp camarones [–oness]
shrink: it's shrunk se ha encogido [seh ah enkoh-*h*eedoh]
shut *(verb)* cerr*a*r [th–]
  shut up! ¡a callar! [ah ka-y*a*r]
shy tímido
sick enfermo [–f*air*–]
  I feel sick estoy mareado [. . . marreh-*a*h-doh]
  he's been sick ha vomitado [ah . . .]
side lado
  side street una callejuela [ka-yeh-*h*weh-la]
  by the side of the road a un lado de la carretera
sidewalk la acera [atheh-ra]
sight: out of sight fuera de la vista [fweh-ra . . .]
  the sights of . . . los lugares de interés de . . . [loss loog*a*ress deh eenter*e*ss]
  sight-seeing tour un recorrido turístico [rekorr*ee*doh toor*ee*steekoh]
sign *(roadsign)* una señal [sen-y*a*l]
  (notice) un letrero
signal: he didn't signal no señaló [noh sen-yalloh]
signature la firma [f*ee*r–]
silence *(noun)* silencio [seelenth-yoh]

silencio *quiet*
silk seda [s*eh*-da]
silly tonto
silver plata
similar parecido [parreh-th*ee*doh]
simple sencillo [senth*ee*yoh]
since: since last week desde la semana pasada
  [d*ez*-deh . . .]
  since we arrived desde que llegamos [. . . keh
  yeh-g*a*h-moss)
  (because) como
sincere sincero [seen-th*eh*-roh]
  yours sincerely le saluda atentamente
sing cant*a*r
single: single room una habitación individual
  [abbee-tath-y*o*n eendee-v*ee*d-w*a*l]
  I'm single estoy soltero
sink: it sank se hundió [seh oond-y*o*h]
sir señor [sen-y*o*r]
sister: my sister mi hermana [mee air-m*a*h-na]
sit: can I sit here? ¿puedo sentarme aquí?
  [pw*eh*-doh sent*a*rmeh ak*ee*]
size talla [t*a*-ya]
ski *(noun)* el esquí [esk*ee*]
  (verb) esquiar [eskee-*a*r]
  ski boots botas de esquí
  skiing el esquí
  ski-lift telesqu*í*
  ski pants pantalones de esquí
  [pantal*o*h-ness . . .]
  ski pole un bast*ó*n de esquí
  ski slope/run una pista [p*ee*sta]
  ski wax cera para esqu*í*es [thera para
  esk*ee*-ess]
skid *(verb)* patin*a*r
skin la piel [pee-*e*ll]
  skin-diving bucear [boo-theh-*a*r]
skirt una falda
sky el cielo [thee-*eh*-loh]
  in the sky en el cielo

sleep: I can't sleep no puedo dormir [noh
    pweh-doh dormeer]
sleeper *(rail)* coche-cama [kotcheh—]
sleeping bag saco de dormir [. . . deh dormeer]
    sleeping pill una pastilla para dormir
    [pass-teeya . . .]
    YOU MAY HEAR . . .
    ¿ha dormido bien? *did you sleep well?*
sleeve la manga
slide *(photographic)* una diapositiva
    [dee-apossee-teeva]
slow lento
    could you speak a little slower? ¿podría
    hablar un poco más despacio? [podree-a ablar
    oon pokoh mass dess-path-yoh]
small pequeño [peckehn-yoh]
    small change calderilla [kaldereeya]
smallpox viruela [veer-weh-la]
smell: there's a funny smell hay un olor raro
    [eye . . .]
    it smells huele mal [weh-leh . . .]
smile *(verb)* sonreír [sonn-reh-eer]
smoke *(noun)* humo [oomoh]
    do you smoke? ¿fuma usted? [fooma oosteh]
    can I smoke? ¿puedo fumar? [pweh-doh
    foomar]
smooth suave [swah-veh]
snack: can we just have a snack? ¿queríamos
    tomar sólo una comida ligera
    [keree-ah-moss . . . kommeeda lee-heh-ra]
snake una serpiente [sair-pee-enteh]
snorkel un respirador
snow nieve [nee-eh-veh]
so: it's so hot hace tanto calor [ah-theh . . .]
    not so much no tanto
    so-so así, así [assee . . .]
soap jabón [habon]
sober sobrio [soh-bree-oh]
sock un calcetín [kal-theh-teen]
soda (water) agua de seltz [ah-gwa deh selts]

soft drink una bebida no alcohólica [beb*ee*da noh alko-*o*lleeka]

sole *(shoe)* suela [sw*eh*-la]

could you put new soles on these? ¿puede ponerles medias suelas? [pw*eh*-deh pon*air*-less m*e*d-yass sw*eh*-lass]

YOU MAY THEN HEAR...

¿de goma o de material? *rubber or leather?*

some: some people algunas personas [alg*oo*nass pair-*s*onass]

can I have some grapes/bread? ¿me pone unas uvas/un poco de pan? [meh p*o*h-neh *oo*nas *oo*vass...]

can I have some more? ¿me pone un poco más? [meh p*o*-neh...]

somebody alguien [*a*lg-yen]

something algo

sometime alguna vez [alg*oo*na veth]

sometimes algunas veces [alg*oo*nass [v*eh*-thess]

somewhere en algún sitio [alg*oo*n s*ee*t-yoh]

son: my son mi hijo [mee *ee-h*oh]

song una canción [kanth-y*o*n]

soon pronto; **sooner** antes [*a*ntess]

as soon as possible lo antes posible [...poss*ee*bleh]

sore: it's sore me duele [meh dw*eh*-leh]

sore throat dolor de garganta

sorry: (I'm) sorry ¡perdón! [pair-d*o*n]

sort: this sort este tipo [*e*ssteh t*ee*poh]

will you sort it out? ¿lo puede arreglar? [loh pw*eh*-deh...]

sótano basement

soup sopa

sour agrio [*a*h-gree-oh]

south sur [soor]

South Africa Sudáfrica [sood−]

South African sudafricano

souvenir un recuerdo [rekw*air*-doh]

spade una pala

spaghetti espaguetis [−gh*e*tteess]

Spain España [esp*a*n-ya]

Spaniard un español [espan-yol]
Spanish español
  a Spanish woman una española
  [espan-yoh-la]
  the Spanish los españoles [espan-yoh-less]
  I don't speak Spanish no hablo español [noh
  *a*h-bloh . . .]
spare: spare part una pieza de repuésto
  [pee-*e*h-tha deh rep*w*esstoh]
  spare wheel rueda de recambio [rw*e*h-da deh
  rek*a*mb-yoh]
spark plug una bujía [boo-*hee*-a]
speak: do you speak English? ¿habla inglés?
  [*a*h-bla eengl*e*ss]
  I don't speak . . . no hablo . . . [noh *a*h-bloh]
special especial [esspeth-y*a*l]
specialist especialista [esspeth-yal*ee*sta]
specially especialm*e*nte [−teh]
speed velocidad [velothee-d*a*]
  he was speeding iba con exceso de velocidad
  [*ee*ba kon ess-th*e*ssoh . . .]
  speed limit límite de velocidad
  [*lee*meeteh . . .]
  speedometer el cuentakilómetros
  [kwenta-kee-l*o*mmetross]
spend *(money)* gastar
spice una especia [esspeth-ya]
  is it spicy? ¿es picante? [. . . peek*a*nteh]
  it's too spicy es demasiado picante
  [. . . demass-y*a*h-doh . . .]
spider una araña [ar*a*hn-ya]
spirits licores [leek*o*ress]
spoon una cuchara [koo−]
sprain: I've sprained my . . . me he torcido
  el . . . [meh eh torth*ee*doh . . .]
spring *(water)* un manantial [−y*a*l]
  (season) la primavera [preema-v*e*h-ra]
  (of car, seat, etc.) un muelle [mw*e*h-yeh]
square *(in town)* una plaza [−tha]
  two square meters dos metros cuadrados
  [. . . kwadr*a*h-doss]

....

stairs la escalera
stale duro [dooroh]
stall: it keeps stalling no hace más que calarse [noh ah-theh mass keh kalar-seh]
stalls butacas de patio [bootah-kass deh pat-yoh]
stamp un sello [seh-yoh]
    two stamps for the U.S. dos sellos para Estados Unidos
» *TRAVEL TIP: stamps are usually bought at "estancos" (tobacco shops); look for red and yellow stripes around entrance*
stand *(verb)* estar de pie [. . . pee-eh]
    (noun: at fair) un stand
standard *(adjective)* normal
star una estrella [esstreh-ya]
starboard estribor
start el comienzo [kom-yenthoh]
    my car won't start mi coche no arranca [mee kotcheh noh . . .]
    when does it start? ¿cuándo empieza? [kwandoh emp-yetha]
starter *(car)* el motor de arranque [. . . deh arrankeh]
starving: I'm starving estoy muerto de hambre [. . . mwairtoh deh ambreh]
station la estación [esstath-yon]
statue una estatua [esstat-wa]
stay: we enjoyed our stay hemos disfrutado mucho de nuestra estancia [eh-moss deesfrootah-doh mootchoh deh nwesstra estanth-ya]
    stay there quédese ahí [keh-deh-seh ah-ee]
    I'm staying at . . . estoy en . . .
    can we stay here? ¿podemos cobijarnos aquí? [podeh-moss kobee-harnoss akee]
steak un filete [feeleh-teh]
    YOU MAY HEAR . . .
    ¿muy hecho? [mwee-etchoh] *well done?*
    ¿poco hecho? *rare?*
    if you like it medium ask for "normal"
steep empinado

steering *(car)* la dirección [deerekth-yon]
  steering wheel el volante [–teh]
step *(noun: of stair)* un escalón
stereo estéreo [essteh-reh-oh]
stewardess la azafata [atha–]
sticky pegajoso [–hosoh]
stiff *(door, etc.)* duro [doo-roh]
still *(adjective)* **keep still** estése quieto
  [essteh-seh kee-eh-toh]
  I'm still here todavía estoy aquí [toda-vee-a
  esstoy akee]
stink *(noun)* mal olor
stolen: my wallet's been stolen me han robado
  la cartera [meh an . . .]
stomach el estómago
  I've got a stomach-ache me duele el vientre
  [meh dweh-leh el vee-entreh]
  **have you got something for an upset
  stomach?** ¿tiene algo para el dolor de
  estómago? [tee-eh-neh . . .]
stone una piedra [pee-eh-dra]
stop: stop! ¡detengase! [deh-tenga-seh]
  stop-over una escala
  do you stop near . . . ? ¿para usted cerca
  de . . . ? [pah-ra oosteh thairka deh]
storm una tormenta
stove una cocina [kotheena]
straight derecho
  go straight on siga derecho [seega . . .]
  straight whisky un whisky solo
strange *(odd)* extraño [esstran-yoh]
  (unknown) desconocido [–theedoh]
stranger un desconocido
  I'm a stranger here soy forastero aquí
  [. . . akee]
strap correa [korreh-a]
strawberry una fresa [freh-sa]
street una calle [ka-yeh]
string: have you got any string? ¿tiene usted
  cuerda? [tee-eh-neh oosteh kwairda]
striptease estriptis [esstreepteess]

....

stroke: he's had a stroke ha sufrido un infarto [ah soof*ree*doh . . .]

strong fuerte [f*wai*rteh]

student estudiante [esstood-y*a*nteh]

stung: I've been stung (by a jellyfish) me ha picado (una medusa) [meh ah peek*a*h-doh oona med*oo*sa]

stupid estúpido [–*too*–]

such: such a lot tanto

suddenly de repente [deh reh-p*e*nteh]

sugar azúcar [ath*oo*–]

suit un traje [tr*a*h-*h*eh]

   suitcase una maleta [–l*eh*–]

suitable adecuado [adek*wa*h-doh]

summer verano [ver*a*h-noh]

sun el sol

   in the sun al sol

   out of the sun a la sombra

   sunbathe tomar el sol

   sunburn una quemadura sol*a*r [keh-mad*oo*ra . . .]

   sunglasses unas gafas de sol

   suntan un bronceado [bronteh-*a*h-doh]

   sunstroke una insolación [–*a*th-yon]

   suntan oil un bronceador [bronteh-ad*o*r]

Sunday domingo

supermarket un supermerc*a*do [–m*ai*r–]

sure: I'm not sure no estoy seguro

   sure! ¡claro que sí! [. . . keh see]

   are you sure? ¿está usted seguro? [oosteh seg*oo*roh]

surfboard plancha de hacer surf [. . . ath-*ai*r soorf]; **to go surfing** ir a hacer surf [eer ah ath*ai*r . . .]

surname apellido [appeh-y*ee*doh]

swearword un taco

sweat *(verb)* sud*a*r [soo–]

sweet: it's too sweet es demasiado dulce [demass-y*a*h-doh d*oo*ltheh]

   (dessert) postre [p*o*ss-treh]

swerve: I had to swerve tuve que torcer

bruscamente [tooveh keh torth-air brooskamenteh]

swim: I'm going for a swim me voy a dar un baño [. . . ban-yoh]

   swimsuit el traje de baño [trah-heh deh ban-yoh]

   let's go for a swim vamos a bañarnos [bah-moss ah ban-yarnoss]

   swimming pool una piscina [peess-theena]

switch *(noun)* el interruptor [−roop−]

   to switch on/off encender/apagar [enthend-air . . .]

table una mesa [meh-sa]

   a table for 4 una mesa para cuatro personas [. . . kwatroh pair− . . .]

   table wine vino de mesa

tailor sastre

take coger [kohair]

   can I take this with me? ¿puedo llevarme esto? [pweh-doh yeh-var-meh . . .]

   will you take me to the airport? ¿quiere llevarme al aeropuerto? [keeeh-reh . . . ah-airo-pwairtoh]

   how long will it take? ¿cuánto tiempo tardará? [kwantoh tee-empoh . . .]

   somebody has taken my bags se han llevado mis maletas [seh an yeh-vah-doh meess . . .]

   can I take you out tonight? ¿quieres salir conmigo esta noche? [kee-eh-ress saleer konmeegoh essta notcheh]

   is this seat taken? ¿está ocupado este asiento? [. . . ass-yentoh]

talcum powder polvos de talco

talk *(verb)* hablar [ablar]

tall alto

tampons tampones [−oness]

tan un bronceado [brontheh-ah-doh]

   I want to get a tan quiero broncearme [kee-eh-roh brontheh-armeh]

tank *(of car)* el depósito [deh-possee-toh]

tape una cinta [th*ee*nta]
tape recorder un magnetofón
taquilla *ticket office*
tariff la tarifa [−r*ee*−]
taste *(noun)* sabor
  can I taste it? ¿puedo probarlo? [pw*eh*-doh . . .]
  it tastes horrible/very nice sabe a
  rayos/muy bien [s*a*h-beh ah r*a*-yoss/mwee
  bee-*e*n]
taxi un taxi
  will you get me a taxi? ¿quiere buscarme un
  taxi? [kee-*e*h-reh boosk*a*rmeh . . .]
  where can I get a taxi? ¿dónde puedo coger
  un taxi? [d*o*ndeh pw*eh*-doh koh*ai*r . . .]
  taxi driver el taxista [−*ee*sta]
tea té [teh]
  could I have a cup of tea? ¿me pone un té,
  por favor? [meh poneh . . .]
» *TRAVEL TIP: unless you ask otherwise, tea is*
  normally served without milk; if you want it
  with milk say "con leche" [kon leh-cheh]
  YOU MAY HEAR . . .
  ¿con limón? *with lemon?*
teach: could you teach me? ¿podría
  enseñarme? [podr*ee*-a ensen-y*a*rmeh]
  could you teach me Spanish? ¿podría
  enseñarme español? [. . . ess-pan-yol]
teacher el profesor
telegram un telegr*a*ma
  I want to send a telegram quiero mand*a*r un
  telegrama [kee-*e*h-roh . . .]
telephone *(noun)* el teléfono [tell*e*ffonoh]
  can I make a phone call? ¿puedo hacer una
  llamada telefónica? [pw*eh*-doh ath-*ai*r oona
  yam*a*h-da . . .]
  can I speak to . . . ? ¿se puede poner . . . ? [seh
  pw*eh*-deh pon*ai*r]
  could you get the number for me? *(dial)*
  ¿podría marcarme usted el número? [podr*ee*-a
  mark*a*r-meh oost*e*h el n*oo*meh-roh]

telephone booth una cabina telefónica
[. . . teh-leh-fonnee-ka]
telephone directory la guía telefónica [ghee-a
tellefonneeka]
» *TRAVEL TIP: money in first, then dial; unused
coins will be returned; code for US is 001, wait
for high-pitched tone.*
television la televisión [–vees-yon]
I'd like to watch television quisiera ver la
televisión [kees-yeh-ra vair la tellevees-yon]
tell: could you tell me where . . . ? ¿podría
decirme dónde . . . ? [podree-a detheer-meh
dondeh]
temperature *(weather, etc.)* la temperatura
[–toora]
tennis el tenis [teh-neess]
tennis court una pista de tenis [peesta . . .]
tennis racket una raqueta de tenis
[rackeh-ta . . .]
tennis ball una pelota de tenis
tent una tienda de campaña [tee-enda deh
kampan-ya]
terminal la estación terminal [estath-yon
tairmeenal]
terrible terrible [terreebleh]
terrific fabuloso [–boo–]
than que [keh]
bigger than más grande que [. . . –deh . . .]
fewer than 5 menos de cinco [meh-noss deh
theenkoh]
thanks, thank you gracias [grath-yass]
no thank you no gracias
thank you very much muchas gracias
thank you for your help gracias por su
ayuda
YOU MAY THEN HEAR . . .
de nada *you're welcome*
that: that man/that table ese hombre/esa mesa
[eh-seh ombreh/eh-sa meh-sa]
I would like that one quiero ese [kee-eh-roh
eh-seh]

....

how do you say that? ¿cómo se dice eso?
[. . . seh deetheh eh-soh]
I think that . . . creo que . . . [kreh-oh keh]
the *(singular)* el; la *(plural)* los; las
theater el teatro [teh-ah-troh]
their su; sus [soo; sooss]
it's their bag, it's theirs es su bolso, es (el)
suyo [. . . sooyo]
them *(objects)* los; las
(persons) les [less]
with/for them con/para ellos [. . . eh-yoss]
who?–them ¿quiénes?–ellos
then entonces [enton-thess]
there allí [a-yee]
how do I get there? ¿cómo se llega? [. . . seh
yeh-ga]
is there . . . /are there . . . ? ¿hay . . . ? [eye]
there you are *(giving something)* tome
[toh-meh]
thermos bottle un termo [tair-moh]
these estos; estas
can I take these? ¿puedo coger éstos?
[pweh-doh kohair esstoss]
they ellos; ellas [eh-yoss/eh-yass]
they are son, están
thick grueso [grweh-soh]
thief un ladrón
thigh el muslo [moozloh]
thin delgado
thing una cosa
I've lost all my things he perdido todas mis
cosas [eh pairdeedoh . . .]
think pensar
I'll think it over lo pensaré [. . . pensareh]
I think so/I don't think so creo que sí/no
creo [kreh-oh keh see . . .]
third *(adjective)* tercero [tair-theh-roh]
thirsty: I'm thirsty tengo sed [. . . seth]
this este; esta
this hotel/this street este hotel/esta calle
[essteh o-tel/esta ka-yeh]

can I have this one? ¿me da éste?
this is my wife/this is Mr. ... ésta es mi
mujer/éste es el señor ... [... mee
moo-*hair* ...]
is this ...? ¿es esto ...?
those esos; esas
how much are those? ¿cuánto valen esos?
[kw*a*ntoh v*a*h-len *e*h-soss]
thread *(noun)* hilo [*ee*loh]
throat la garganta
throttle *(motorcycle, boat)* el acelerador
[atheh-leh-rad*o*r]
through a través de [ah travess deh]
throw *(verb)* tir*a*r [tee−]
thumb el dedo pulgar [d*e*h-doh poolg*a*r]
thumbtack una chincheta
thunder *(noun)* un trueno [trweh-noh]
thunderstorm una tormenta
Thursday jueves [*h*weh-vess]
ticket *(train, bus, plane, boat)* un billete
[beey*e*h-teh]
(movie) una entrada
(coatroom) un ticket [*tee*-keh]
ticket office el despacho de billetes [... deh
bee-y*e*h-tess]
tie *(necktie)* una corbata
tight *(clothes)* ajustado [a*h*oos−]
they're too tight son demasiado ajustados
[demass-y*a*h-doh a*h*oosst*a*h-doss]
tights unos leotardos [*oo*noss leh-o-t*a*rdoss]
time el tiempo [tee-*e*mpoh]
what time is it? ¿qué hora es? [keh *o*ra ess]
I haven't got time no tengo tiempo
for the time being por el momento
this time/last time/next time esta vez/la
*ú*ltima vez/la pr*ó*xima vez [... veth]
three times tres veces [tress vethess]
have a good time! ¡que se divierta! [keh seh
deev-y*ai*rta]
timetable el horario [or-*a*r-yoh]

» *TRAVEL TIP: how to tell the time*
it's one o'clock es la una [oona]
it's two/three/four o'clock son las
dos/tres/cuatro [doss/tress/kwatroh]
it's 5/10/20/25 past seven son las siete y
cinco/diez/veinte/veinticinco [ee theenkoh/dee-
eth/vainteh/vaintee-theenkoh]
it's quarter past eight/eight fifteen son las
ocho y cuarto [ee kwartoh]
it's half past nine/nine thirty son las nueve
y media [nweh-veh ee maid-ya]
it's 25/20/10/5 to ten son las diez menos
veinticinco/veinte/diez/cinco [meh-noss]
it's quarter to eleven/10:45 son las once
menos cuarto [ontheh meh-noss kwartoh]
it's twelve o'clock (am/pm) son las doce [de
la mañana/de la noche) [doh-theh deh la
man-yah-na/deh la notcheh]
at one o'clock a la una [ah . . .]
at three thirty a las tres y media [ah lass
tress ee maid-ya]
tip *(noun)* una propina [–pee–]
is the tip included? ¿va incluída la propina?
[. . . eenklweeda . . .]
» *TRAVEL TIP: 10% is usual; tip same people as in
US; but usherettes will also expect a tip*
tire una rueda [rweh-da]
I need a new tire necesito una rueda nueva
[nethesseetoh oona rweh-da nweh-va]
» *TRAVEL TIP: tire pressures*

lb/sq. in.	18	20	22	24	26	28	30
kg/sq. cm	1.3	1.4	1.5	1.7	1.8	2	2.1

tired cansado
I'm tired estoy cansado
tissues kleenex
to: to Madrid/U.S. a Madrid/Estados Unidas [ah
madree . . .]
toast una tostada
(drinking) un brindis [breendeess]
tobacco tabaco
tobacco shop el estanco

today hoy [oy]
toe un dedo del pie [d*e*h-doh del pee-*e*h]
together junto [*hoon*toh]
    we're together venimos juntos [ven*ee*moss . . .]
    can we pay all together? ¿puede cobrarlo
    todo junto? [pw*e*h-deh . . .]
toilet los aseos [ass-*e*h-oss]
    where are the toilets? ¿dónde están los
    aseos?
    I have to go to the toilet tengo que ir al
    wáter [. . . keh eer al v*a*ttair]
    there's no toilet paper no hay papel
    higiénico [no eye pap*e*l ee*h*-yeh-neekoh]
    public restroom aseos públicos
    [ass-*e*h-oss . . .]
    men's room los servicios de caballeros
    ladies' room los aseos de señoras
» *TRAVEL TIP: not many public toilets; usually in
    stations; don't hesitate to go into a bar or café
    and use their toilet*
tomato tomate [toh-m*a*h-teh]
    tomato juice zumo de tomate [th*oo*-moh . . .]
tomorrow mañana [man-y*a*h-na]
    **tomorrow morning/tomorrow afternoon/
    tomorrow evening** mañana por la
    mañana/mañana por la tarde/mañana por la
    noche [. . . t*a*rdeh/ . . . notcheh]
    the day after tomorrow pasado mañana
    see you tomorrow hasta mañana
    [*a*sta . . .]
ton una tonelada [tonneh-l*a*h-da]
» *TRAVEL TIP: 1 ton = 1,016 kilos*
tongue la lengua [l*e*ng-gwa]
tonic (water) tónica
tonight esta noche [. . . n*o*tcheh]
tonsils las amígdalas [am*ee*gdalass]
tonsillitis amigdalitis [−*ee*teess]
too demasiado [demass-y*a*h-doh] *(also)* también
    [tamb-y*e*n]
    that's too much eso es demasiado
tool una herramienta [erram-y*e*nta]

tooth un diente [dee-*enteh*]
  (back teeth) las muelas [mweh-lass]
  I've got a toothache tengo dolor de muelas
  toothbrush un cepillo de dientes [thepp*ee*yoh]
  toothpaste pasta dentífrica [. . . dent*ee*freeka]
top: on top of . . . encima de [enth*ee*ma deh]
  on the top floor en el *ú*ltimo piso [. . . p*ee*-soh]
  at the top en lo alto
torch una linterna [leent*ai*rna]
total *(noun)* el total
tough *(meat)* dura [d*oo*ra]
tour *(noun)* un viaje [vee-ah-*h*eh]
  we'd like to go on a tour of . . . nos gustaría
  hacer un viaje por . . . [noss goostar*ee*-a
  ath-*air* . . .]
  package tour un viaje organizado [oom
  bee-*ah*-*h*eh organeeth*ah*-doh]
tourist turista [tur*ee*ss-ta]
  I'm a tourist soy un turista
  tourist office la oficina de turismo
  [offeeth*ee*na deh toor*ee*zmoh]
tow *(verb)* remolcar
  can you give me a tow? ¿puede usted
  remolcarme? [pweh-deh oosteh . . .]
  towrope un cable de remolque [k*ah*-bleh deh
  remol-keh]
towards hacia [*ath*-ya]
  he was coming straight towards me venía
  derecho hacia mí [ven*ee*-a derecho *ath*-ya mee]
towel una toalla [toh-*ah*-ya]
town una ciudad [thee-ood*a*]
  (smaller) un pueblo [pweh-bloh]
  in town en el centro [. . . th*e*ntroh]
  would you take me into the town? ¿podría
  llevarme al centro? [podr*ee*-a yeh-v*ar*-meh . . .]
traditional tradicional [tradeeth-yon*a*l]
  a traditional Spanish meal una comida
  española tradicional [. . . komm*ee*da . . .]
traffic el tráfico
  traffic lights los sem*á*foros

traffic policeman un guardia de la
circulación [gwar-dee-a deh la
theer-koo-lath-yon]

train el tren
» *TRAVEL TIP: important to reserve in advance as
trains tend to be crowded; train travel is slow*

tranquilizers calmantes [–tess]

translate traducir [–ootheer]
  would you translate that for me? ¿quiere
  usted traducirme eso, por favor? [kee-eh-reh
  oosteh tradootheer-meh . . .]

transmission *(of car)* la transmisión [trans-
meess-yon]

travel:

travel agency una agencia de viajes [ahenth-ya
deh vee-ah-hess]
  we're traveling around estamos de turismo
  [. . . tooreezmoh]

traveler's check un cheque de viaje [cheh-keh
deh vee-ah-heh]

tree un árbol

tremendous tremendo

trim: just a trim please recórtemelo nada más,
por favor [reh-korteh-meh-loh . . .]

trip *(noun)* una excursión [ess-koors-yon]
  we want to go on a trip to . . . queremos
  hacer una excursión a . . . [kereh-moss
  ath-air . . .]
  have a good trip! ¡buen viaje! [bwem-
  bee-aheh]

trouble *(noun)* problemas
  I'm having trouble with . . . estoy teniendo
  problemas con . . . [. . . ten-yendoh
  probleh-mass . . .]

trousers unos pantalones [–loh-ness]

truck un camión [kam-yon]
  truck driver un camionero [kam-yoneh-roh]

true verdadero [vair-dadeh-roh]
  it's not true no es verdad [. . . vair-da]

trunk *(car)* el portaequipajes
[porta-eckee-pahess]

trunks *(swimming)* un bañador (de hombre)
[ban-ya-d*o*r deh *o*mbreh]
try *(verb)* intent*a*r
  please try haga el favor de intentarlo
  [*a*h-ga . . .]
  can I try? ¿puedo prob*a*r yo? [pweh-doh . . .]
  can I try it on? ¿puedo probármelo?
  [pweh-doh proh-b*a*r-meh-loh]
T-shirt una camiseta [kamee-s*e*h-ta]
Tuesday martes [−tess]
tunnel un túnel [t*o*onell]
turn: where do we turn off? ¿dónde tenemos
  que desviarnos? [d*o*ndeh ten-*e*h-moss keh
  dess-vee-*a*rnoss]
  he turned without signaling giró sin
  señalar [h*e*e-roh seen sen-yal*a*r]
twice dos veces [. . . v*e*thess]
  twice as much dos veces más
twin beds dos camas
two dos [doss]
typewriter una máquina de escribir [m*a*ckeena
  deh esskreeb*e*er]
typical típico [t*e*e−]
ugly feo [f*e*h-oh]
ulcer una úlcera [*o*ol-theh-ra]
umbrella un paraguas [par*a*hg-wass]
uncle: my uncle mi tío [mee t*e*e-oh]
uncomfortable incómodo
unconscious inconsciente [−sthee-*e*nteh]
under debajo de [deb*a*h-*h*oh deh]
underdone poco hecho [. . . *e*tchoh]
underground *(rail)* el metro
understand: I understand lo comprendo
  I don't understand no entiendo [noh
  ent-y*e*ndoh]
  do you understand? ¿entiende usted?
  [ent-y*e*ndeh oost*e*h]
underwear *(shorts)* los calzoncillos
  [kalthon-th*e*eyoss]
undo deshacer [dess-ath-*a*ir]
unfriendly antipático [antee-p*a*ttekoh]

unhappy desgraciado [dess-grath-y*a*h-doh]
United States Estados Unidos [esst*a*h-doss
  oon*ee*doss]
unleaded sin plomo [seen pl*o*moh]
unlock abrir [abr*ee*r]
until hasta que [*a*sta keh]
  until next year hasta el año que viene [*a*sta
  el *a*n-yoh keh vee-eh-neh]
unusual poco corriente [. . . korr-y*e*nteh]
up arriba [arr*ee*ba]
  he's not up yet todavía no se ha levantado
  [toh-dav*ee*-a noh seh ah . . .]
  what's up? ¿qué pasa? [keh . . .]
upside down al revés [al reh-v*e*ss]
upstairs arriba [arr*ee*ba]
urgent urgente [oor-*h*enteh]
us nos [noss]
  with/for us con/para nosotros
  [. . . noss*o*h-tross]
  who?–us ¿quiénes?–nosotros
use: can I use . . . ? ¿puedo usar . . . ? [pweh-doh
  oos*a*r]
useful útil [*oo*teel]
usual habitual [abbeet-w*a*l]
  as usual como de costumbre [. . . deh
  koss-t*oo*m-breh]
usually normalm*e*nte [–teh]
U-turn un viraje en U [veer*a*h-*h*eh en oo]
**vacancy: do you have any
  vacancies?** *(hotel)* ¿tiene alguna habitación
  libre? [tee-eh-neh alg*oo*na abbee-tath-yon
  l*ee*breh]
vacate *(room)* desocupar [–koo–]
vacation vacaciones [vacath-yoness]
  I'm on vacation estoy de vacaciones
vaccination una vacuna [–koo–]
valid válido
  how long is it valid for? ¿hasta cuándo tiene
  validez? [*a*sta kwandoh tee-eh-neh valeed*e*th]
valley un valle [v*a*-yeh]
valuable valioso [val-y*o*soh]

will you look after my valuables? ¿quiere cuidar de mis objetos de valor? [kee-*e*h-reh kweed*a*r deh meess ob-*h*eh-toss deh val*o*r]

value *(noun)* valor

valve una v*á*lvula [−voo−]

van una furgoneta [foor-gonn*e*h-ta]

vanilla vainilla [vye-n*ee*yah]

varicose veins varices [var*ee*thess]

Vd., Vds.* = *usted, ustedes* *you

veal ternera [tair-n*e*h-rah]

vegetables verduras [vair-d*oo*rass]

vegetarian *(noun)* vegetariano [ve*h*etarree-*a*h-noh]

***velocidad limitada* speed limit**

***venta de sellos* stamps**

ventilator el ventilad*o*r

very muy [mwee]

　　very much mucho [moo−]

via por

village un pueblo [pw*e*h-bloh]

vine una vid [v*ee*the]

vinegar vinagre [veen*a*h-greh]

vineyard un viñedo [veen-y*e*h-doh]

vintage cosecha

　　vintage wine vino añejo [v*ee*no an-y*e*h-*h*oh]

violent violento [vee-o-l*e*ntoh]

visibility visibilidad [veeseebeeleed*a*]

visit *(verb)* visitar [veeseet*a*r]

vodka vodka

voice una voz [voth]

voltage voltaje [voll-t*a*h-*h*eh]

waist la cintura [theent*oo*ra]

» *TRAVEL TIP: waist measurements*

US	24	26	28	30	32	34	36	38
Spain	61	66	71	76	80	87	91	97

wait: will we have to wait long? ¿tendremos que esperar mucho? [tendr*e*h-moss keh esspeh-r*a*r m*o*ochoh]

　　wait for me espéreme [essp*e*h-reh-meh]

　　I'm waiting for a friend/my wife estoy

esperando a un amigo/a mi mujer [. . . mee
moo-*hair*]

waiter un camarero [–*reh*-roh]
  waiter! ¡camarero!
» *TRAVEL TIP: it's not rude to click your fingers to
  get the waiter*

waitress una camarera
  waitress! ¡señorita! [sen-yor*ee*ta]

wake: will you wake me up at 7:30? ¿quiere
  despertarme a las siete y media? [kee-*eh*-reh
  dess-pair-*tar*meh ah lass see-*eh*-teh ee m*ai*d-ya]

Wales Gales [*gah*-less]

walk: can we walk there? ¿se puede ir a pie?
  [seh pw*eh*-deh eer ah pee-*eh*]
  **are there any good walks around
  here?** ¿hay algún sitio bonito por donde
  pasear aqui? [alg*oon* s*ee*t-yoh bonn*ee*toh por
  d*on*deh passeh-*ar* ak*ee*]
  walking shoes zapatos de campo
  [thap*ah*-toss . . .]

wall una pared [par*eh*h]

wallet la cartera [kart*eh*-ra]

want: I want a . . . ¿quiero un/una . . .
  [kee-*eh*-roh . . .]
  I want to talk to . . . quiero hablar con . . .
  [kee-*eh*-roh abl*ar* . . .]
  what do you want? ¿qué quiere usted? [keh
  kee-*eh*-reh oost*eh*]
  I don't want to no quiero (hacerlo) [noh
  kee-*eh*-roh ath-*air*-loh]
  he wants to . . . quiere . . .

warm: it's warm today hoy hace calor [oy
  ah-theh . . .]
  I feel very warm tengo mucho calor

warning aviso [av*ee*soh]

was: I was/he was (yo) era; estaba/(él) era;
  estaba
  it was era; estaba [*eh*-ra . . .]

wash: can you wash these for me? ¿podría
  lavármelos? [podr*ee*-a lav*ar*-meh-loss]

where can I wash...? ¿dónde puedo
lavar...? [dondeh pweh-doh...]
  washing machine una lavadora
washer *(for bolt, etc.)* una arandela
wasp una avispa [−vee−]
watch *(wrist-)* el reloj [reh-loh]
  will you watch my bags for me? ¿me podría
  vigilar las maletas? [meh podree-a veeheelar]
  watch out! ¡cuidado! [kweedah-doh]
water agua [ahg-wa]
  can I have some water? ¿puede traerme
  agua? [pweh-deh trah-airmeh ahg-wa]
  hot and cold running water agua caliente y
  fría [...kal-yenteh ee free-a]
  waterproof impermeable
  [eempair-meh-ah-bleh]
  waterskiing esquí acuático [esskee
  akwatteekoh]
way: we'd like to eat the Spanish way
  quisiéramos comer a la española
  [keess-yeh-ramoss komair ah la esspan-yola]
  could you tell me the way to...? ¿podría
  indicarme el camino para...? [podree-a...]
  see **where** *for answers*
we nosotros [nossoh-tross]
  we are somos
  we are tired estamos cansados
weak *(person)* débil [deh-beel]
weather el tiempo [tee-empoh]
  what awful weather! ¡qué tiempo tan
  asqueroso! [keh tee-empoh tan asskeh-rosoh]
  what's the weather forecast? ¿cuál es el
  pronóstico del tiempo? [kwal ess...]
  YOU MAY THEN HEAR...
  va a hacer sol [vah-ath-air sol] *it'll be sunny*
  va a llover [...yoh-vair] *it's going to rain*
  va a mejorar el tiempo [...meh-horar el
  tee-empoh] *it'll improve*
Wednesday miércoles [mee-air-koless]
week una semana

a week from today/tomorrow de hoy/de mañana en una semana [deh oy . . .]

at the weekend el fin de semana [el feen . . .]

weight peso [peh-soh]

well: I'm not feeling well no me encuentro bien [noh meh enkwentroh bee-en]

he's not well no está bueno [. . . bweh-noh]

how are you? very well, thanks ¿cómo está usted? muy bien, graciae [. . . oosteh? mwee bee-en grath-yass]

you speak English very well usted habla inglés muy bien [oosteh ah-bla eengless mwee bee-en]

were: you were *(singular)* (tú) eras/estabas; (usted) era/estaba

you were *(plural)* (vosotros) érais/estábais [eh-ra-eess/esstah-bah-eess]; (ustedes) eran/estaban

see **you**

we were (nosotros) éramos/estábamos

they were (ellos) eran/estaban

Welsh galés [galess]

west oeste [o-esteh]

West Indian antillano [anteeyah-noh]

West Indies las Antillas [anteeyass]

wet mojado [mohah-doh]

wet suit un traje isotérmico [trah-heh eesso-tair-meekoh]

what que [keh]

what is that? ¿qué es eso? [keh ess eh-soh]

what for? ¿para qué?

what's that in Spanish? ¿cómo se llama eso en español? [. . . seh yama . . .]

wheel la rueda [roo-eh-da]

wheelchair una silla de inválido [see-yah deh . . .]

when cuando [kwandoh]

when is breakfast? ¿a qué hora es el desayuno? [ah keh ora . . .]

where donde [dondeh]

where is the post office? ¿dónde está la oficina de Correos? [...offeetheena deh korreh-oss]
YOU MAY THEN HEAR...
siga derecho [seega deh-retchoh] *continue straight ahead*
la primera/segunda a la izquierda/derecha [...eeth-kee-airda...] *first/second on the left/right*

which que [keh]
which one? ¿cuál? [kwal]
YOU MAY THEN HEAR...
éste/ésta *this one*
ése/ésa *that one*
aquel/aquella [akell/akeh-ya] *that one there*

whisky whisky
white blanco
who quien [kee-en]
whose cuyo [koo-yoh]
whose is this? ¿de quién es esto? [deh kee-en...]
YOU MAY THEN HEAR...
es mío/es mía [mee-oh/mee-a] *it's mine*

why por qué [...keh]
why not? ¿por qué no?

wide ancho
wife: my wife mi mujer [mee moo-hair]
will: when will it be finished? ¿cuándo estará terminado? [kwandoh esstara tair-meenah-doh]
will you do it? ¿lo puede hacer? [loh pweh-deh ath-air]
I will come back volveré [vol-veh-reh]

win ganar
who won? ¿quién ha ganado? [kee-en ah...]

wind *(noun)* el viento [vee-entoh]
window la ventana
(of shop) el escaparate [−ah-teh]
near the window cerca de la ventana [thairka...]

windshield el parabrisas [parabree-sass]

windshield wipers los limpiaparabrisas
[l*eemp*-ya−]
windy: it's too windy hace demasiado viento
[*a*h-theh demass-yah-doh vee-*e*ntoh]
wine vino
    can I see the wine list? ¿me enseña la lista
de vinos? [meh ens*e*n-ya la l*ee*sta deh v*e*e-noss]
» *TRAVEL TIP:*
    blanco/tinto/rosado: white/red/rosé
    jerez fino/amontillado/oloroso: dry/medium/
    cream sherry
    Jumilla: dry, red wines
    Málaga: very sweet; try Málaga Virgen
    Penedes: good Catalan wines, especially whites
    and sparkling; try Torres
    Rioja: arguably the best, especially reds; try
    Marqués de Cáceres, Privilegio, Cerro Añón,
    Carta de Oro/Berberana
    Váldepeñas: young, mainly red wines
    Sangria: red wine, lemonade, brandy and
    sugar mix, with sliced apple and oranges
winter invierno [eembee-*a*ir-noh]
wire un alambre [−breh]
    (electrical) un cable eléctrico [. . . kah-bleh . . .]
with con
without sin [seen]
witness *(noun)* un testigo [tess*tee*goh]
    will you act as a witness for me? ¿quiere
usted actuar como testigo mío? [kee-*e*h-reh
oost*e*h ak-too-*a*r k*o*moh tess*tee*goh m*e*e-oh]
woman una mujer [moo-*hair*]
    women las mujeres [moo-*he*-ress]
wonderful estupendo [−too−]
won't: it won't start no arranca
wood madera [mad*e*h-ra]
    (forest) un bosque [b*o*sskeh]
wool lana
word una palabra
    I don't know that word no conozco esa
palabra [no kon*o*thko . . .]

....

work *(verb)* trabajar [trabahar]
  it's not working no funciona [foonth-yonah]
  I work in New York trabajo en Nuevo York
  [trabah-hoh]
worry una preocupación [preh-okkoo-path-yon]
  I'm worried about him estoy preocupado
  por él
  don't worry no se preocupe [noh seh
  preh-okoopeh]
worse: it's worse es peor [peh-or]
  he's getting worse está empeorando
worst el peor [peh-or]
worth: it's not worth that much no vale tanto
  [...vah-leh...]
  is it worthwhile going to...? ¿vale la pena
  ir a...? [vah-leh la peh-na eer ah]
wrap: could you wrap it up? ¿me lo envuelve?
  [meh loh embwel-veh]
wrench *(noun: tool)* una llave inglesa [yah-veh
  eengleh-sa]
wrist la muñeca [moon-yeh-ka]
write escribir [esskreebeer]
  could you write it down? ¿puede
  escribírmelo? [pweh-deh esskreebeer-meh-loh]
  I'll write to you le escribiré [leh
  esskreebeereh]
  writing paper papel de escribir
wrong: I think the bill's wrong me parece que
  la cuenta está equivocada [meh pareh-theh keh
  la kwenta esta eh-keevoh-kah-da]
  there's something wrong with... le pasa
  algo a... [leh...ah...]
  you're wrong se equivoca [seh eh-keevoh-ka]
  sorry, wrong number perdone, me he
  equivocado de número [pairdoh-neh, meh eh
  eh-keevo-kah-doh deh noomeh-roh]
X-ray una radiografía [raddee-ografee-a]
yacht un yate [yah-teh]
yard una yarda
» *TRAVEL TIP: 1 yard = 91.44 cm = 0.91 m*
year un año [an-yoh]

this year/next year este año/el año que viene
[. . . keh vee-*eh*-neh]

yellow amarillo [−*eey*oh]

yes sí [see]

yesterday ayer [ah-y*air*]

    the day before yesterday anteayer
[anteh-ah-y*air*]

    yesterday morning/afternoon ayer por la
mañana/tarde [. . . man-y*ah*-na/t*ar*deh]

yet: is it ready yet? ¿está listo ya?

    not yet todavía no [todav*ee*-a]

yogurt yogur [yog*oo*r]

you tú/usted/vosotros/ustedes
[too/oost*eh*/ . . . /oosteh-dess]

    I don't understand you no le entiendo [noh
leh ent-yen-doh]

    with you contigo [−*tee*−]; con usted

    » *TRAVEL TIP: use "usted/ustedes" in most
situations; the forms "tu/vosotros" are only used
for people you know well*

young joven [*h*oh-ven]

your tu/su/vuestro [too/soo/vwesstroh]

    is this your camera? ¿es suya esta máquina?
[ess s*oo*ya *e*sta m*a*ckeena]

    is this yours? ¿es suyo esto? [ess s*oo*yoh . . .]
see **you**

youth hostel albergue juvenil [al-b*air*-gheh
*h*ooveh-n*ee*l]

zero cero [th*eh*-roh]

    below zero bajo cero [b*ah*-*h*oh . . .]

zip una cremallera [kreh-ma-y*eh*-ra]

zona azul restricted parking

....

 0 cero [th*eh*-roh]
 1 uno [*oo*noh]
 2 dos [doss]
 3 tres
 4 cuatro [kw−]
 5 cinco [th*een*-koh]
 6 seis [sayss]
 7 siete [see-*eh*-teh]
 8 ocho
 9 nueve [nw*eh*-veh]
10 diez [dee-*eth*]
11 once [*on*-theh]
12 doce [d*oh*-theh]
13 trece [tr*eh*-theh]
14 catorce [kat*or*-theh]
15 quince [k*een*-theh]
16 dieciseis [dee-*ethee*-s*ayss*]
17 diecisiete [dee-*ethee*-see-*eh*-teh]
18 dieciocho [dee-*ethee*-ochoh]
19 diecinueve [dee-*ethee*-nw*eh*-veh]
20 veinte [v*ain*-teh]
21 veintiuno
22 veintidos
23 veintitres
24 veinticuatro
25 veinticinco
26 veintiseis
27 veintisiete
28 veintiocho
29 veintinueve
30 treinta [tr*ain*-ta]
31 treinta y uno [traint-eye-*oo*noh]
40 cuarenta [kw−]
41 cuarenta y uno [kwar*ent*-eye-*oo*noh]
50 cincuenta [th*een*-kwenta]
51 cincuenta y uno [theen-kw*ent*-eye-*oo*noh]
60 sesenta
61 sesenta y uno [sess*ent*-eye-*oo*noh]
70 setenta
71 setenta y uno [sett*ent*-eye-*oo*noh]
80 ochenta

81 ochenta y uno [ochent-eye-*oo*noh]
90 noventa
91 noventa y uno [novent-eye-*oo*noh]
100 cien [thee-*e*n]
101 ciento uno
165 ciento sesenta y cinco
     [thee-*e*ntoh-sessent-eye-th*e*enkoh]
200 doscientos [doss-thee-*e*ntoss]
300 trescientos [tress-thee-*e*ntoss]
400 cuatrocientos [kwatroh-thee-*e*ntoss]
500 quinientos [keen-y*e*ntoss]
600 seiscientos [sayss-thee-*e*ntoss]
700 setecientos [seh-teh-thee-*e*ntoss]
800 ochocientos [otchoh-thee-*e*ntoss]
900 novecientos [noveh-thee-*e*ntoss]
1,000 mil [meel]
2,000 dos mil
4,653 cuatro mil seiscientos cincuenta y tres
     [kw*a*troh meel sayss-thee-*e*ntoss
     theen-kwent-eye-tr*e*ss]
1,000,000 un millón [meel-yon]

*Note: in Spain the comma is a decimal point; for
thousands use a period, e.g. 3.000*

The alphabet: how to spell in Spanish
a [ah] **b** [beh] **c** [theh] **ch** [cheh] **d** [deh]
e [eh] **f** [eh-feh] **g** [heh] **h** [*a*tcheh] **i** [ee]
j [hoh-ta] **k** [ka] **l** [*e*h-leh] **ll** [*e*h-yeh]
m [*e*h-meh] **n** [*e*h-neh] **ñ** [*e*n-yeh] **o** [oh]
p [peh] **q** [koo] **r** [*e*h-reh] **rr** [*e*rreh]
s [*e*h-seh] **t** [teh] **u** [oo] **v** [*oo*-veh]
w [*oo*-veh d*o*h-bleh] **x** [*e*ckeess]
y [eegree-*e*h-ga] **z** [th*e*h-ta]